A Visit From John Wesley

With Daily Devotionals and Poems of Faith

Don Germano

Parson's Porch Books

A Visit From John Wesley
ISBN: Softcover 978-1-960326-08-9
Copyright © 2023 by Don Germano

Cover Painting of John Wesley by George Romney (English 1734-1802)

Parson's Porch Books is an imprint of Parson's Porch *&* Company (PP*&*C) in Cleveland, Tennessee. PP*&*C is a self-funded charity which earns money by publishing books of noted authors, representing all genres. Its face and voice is **David Russell Tullock** who you can contact at: dtullock@parsonsporch.com.

Parson's Porch *&* Company *turns books into bread & milk* by sharing its profits with the poor.

www.parsonsporch.com

A Visit From John Wesley

For

Sara Mac

Amy and Brian

CONTENTS

A FEW SELECTED DAILY DEVOTIONALS

INTRODUCTION

1984 was the Bi-Centennial Year of the founding of the Methodist Church in America. As a Charter Member of a newly established little Methodist Church, several members of our Sunday School Class were asked to select one of the Founding Fathers of the Methodist Church, John Wesley, Charles Wesley, Francis Asbury, or Thomas Coke, and each to present to our Church a program on one Sunday over a period of a month in celebration of the Bi-Centennial Year. I chose John Wesley, and with a love of the church and a love of history, I read every book I could find on John Wesley, wrote a script, and decided to present my program as a costumed portrayal of John Wesley. That was the beginning of almost forty years of portraying John Wesley to churches throughout the North and South Georgia Conferences of the United Methodist Church, as well as a few in North Carolina. One weekend, I presented my portrayal of John Wesley to the United Methodist Men of the North Georgia Conference at their assemblage at Rock Eagle near Eatonton, Georgia.

With that same love of history, I also created and presented other costumed portrayals, including those of Abraham Lincoln, Thomas Jefferson, and Patrick Henry, and presented them to church groups, schools, civic clubs and organizations throughout the Metropolitan Atlanta and North Georgia area.

Don Germano

John Wesley

A VISIT FROM JOHN WESLEY

Pardon me for interrupting! I was riding outside on horseback when I heard someone mention John Wesley. Well, I know a little about that subject! For those of you who don't know me, let me introduce myself. My name is John Wesley! There are those that say that I was the founder of this religious sect called "Methodist." Well, I don't know about that! I know I never intended to be the founder of a new church, nor a new denomination. In fact, throughout my life I remained a loyal priest of the Church of England. Yet I found little comfort in the established Church of England, and I found little satisfaction there. I guess you might say that I did what I had to do, at least I did what I was called upon to do by God! And that consisted primarily of two things: One of preaching the Gospel and spreading the Good News to those who had not been reached by the established Church of England and its priests, and secondly, by caring and ministering to those who had already found a Christian life.

Now in order for you to understand me a little better. I thought I might tell you a little about my life. You see, I was born in Epworth, in Lincolnshire England in 1703. I was the fifteenth of nineteen children born of Samuel and Susanna Wesley! My father, Samuel Wesley, was also a Priest of the Church of England. He had been a "Dissenter" or a "non-Conformist" at one time. He was the Rector there at Epworth! Now I know you're going to find this hard to believe in view of the very large size of my family, and yet it's true, that my father spent very little time at home. And the time that he did spend at home, they say he spent in scholarly endeavor! Well, I don't know about that, but I do know that I learned a great deal from my father. I learned from my father a love of God, a love of religion, and a love of the Church! I learned from my father a respect for Orthodoxy, and a respect for the Church of England! I learned from my father self-discipline, as well as from my mother. And last, but not least, I learned from my father a love of learning, a love of the scholarly endeavor if you please.

Now my mother Susanna! Ah, my mother Susanna! I guess of all the individuals that had any influence on my life, my mother was the greatest! My mother herself was the twenty-fifth child of her father and coming from a very large family she had learned at a very early age the importance of tight control within a large family. And our family being very large, and my father being away from home for lengthy periods of time, my mother did run our family with very tight control! She ran it almost as if it were a military unit. Each child had his assigned duties and tasks, and we did those assigned duties and tasks without grumbling! There was no way we were going to grumble, or not do our jobs there at the Wesley household! By the time we were one year of age, we had learned to respect the rod, and if to cry, if at all, to cry very softly! And by the time we were five years of age, we were all given an examination by our mother to see if we had learned the alphabet. All but two of the children had learned their letters by their fifth birthday, and having learned our letters we were handed a book and expected to learn to read. I say we were handed **a** book, we were handed **"The Book"**, for the Holy Bible was our primary and principal text, and beginning at age six, we studied six hours a day with our mother as our tutor and the Bible as our primary text, and this continued until we were ten years of age, at which time the boys went off to boarding school, and the girls stayed home and continued to learn and study from their mother those things that were so important to a woman of that day and time!

Now I do remember a couple of things about my childhood: One, although my mother was very busy with this very large family, she did find time to spent one hour alone a week with each of the children. This was very precious, very meaningful time, a time for learning, a time for sharing, a time when we could talk with our mother about anything that was on our minds!

My second memory was not as pleasant! It was very late at night, we had all gone to bed, when suddenly there were shouts of fire throughout the house. All my brothers and sisters had managed to

16

get out of the house by scrambling out of windows and doors. I had not heard the cries of fire in time and had become trapped on the second floor of our two-story framed house. My father had tried to rescue me, but by the time he had accounted for the other children, the entire house was engulfed in fire. In fact my father had thought I had been taken by the fire, and as he gathered my mother and my brothers and sisters around him, he knelt in prayer and was commending my soul to God when suddenly they heard my cries for help from a second story window, and rushing to my rescue, they first tried a make-shift ladder, which quickly broke. Then two villagers stood on each other's shoulders and grabbed me from that second story window just moments before the roof caved in and the entire house went up in flames. I know my mother said after that, that she was going to pay particular attention to the soul of this child who had been so mercifully spared by God from for some special purpose in life, and I always said after that, that "I was a brand plucked from the burning!"

Well, getting back to my education, I was no exception! At age ten, I went off to boarding school. I went to Charter House there in London where I completed my formal secondary education at seventeen years of age, and then I continued with my education by going to Christ Church Collage there at Oxford. I had known for a long time that I wanted to be a priest of the Church of England, so I went to Oxford to study for the ministry. I was a good student! I studied very hard, and after four years I graduated with very high honors, became a Deacon, and later was ordained as a Priest of the Church of England. Since I had no parish of my own, I began working with my father at his assistant at his church for a couple of years, and then I continued with my education by going back to Christ Church College. Now by this time my brother Charles, who I'm sure you've heard of, was already there. Well, he and some other students, including a young man by the name of George Whitfield, (by the way, George Whitfield, was a young, enthusiastic student of the priesthood. He was a great orator and had what I guess you might call today "charisma"), well, together we formed what was called by the other students, "The Holy Club!" But we were very serious! We would rise at 5:00 in the morning, we would say our prayers and meditations throughout the day, we fasted a couple of times a week and took Holy Communion a couple of times a week, and because we were so "methodical" in our devotions, the other students jokingly called us, "Methodist," because of our methods, and the methodical way we conducted ourselves and our devotions. And we became known as "Methodist," a name that stuck with us, and a name I guess we share in common here today!

Well by 1730, we "Methodist" had begun doing social work. We would go out into the prisons, help the prisoners learn to read and help them find jobs. We would go out into the community and help the poor, providing them with food, clothing, shelter, and books. We even established a couple of schools for the poor and needy children in our community, all the time preaching the Gospel in our humble fashion!

By the time my college days had ended, I thought my work was ended and so we disbanded the Holy Club, but in reality, the spark of Methodism had already begun! We had already started doing those things that Methodist do, in gathering together in Christian fellowship, in preaching the Gospel and spreading the "Good News" of salvation by faith and helping the poor and the needy. By this time, my father had died, and I had no parish of my own so I began going out and preaching whenever and wherever I could. I know I would go out on little mission trips. On one such mission trip I went to London where I preached for some period of time. While in London I had the good fortune of becoming good friends with Colonel James Oglethorpe, perhaps you have heard of him. Colonel Oglethorpe had won fame on the military battlefields of Germany. He had fought under the famous Duke of Marlborough, but by this time Colonel Oglethorpe was tired and weary of war! He had the noble idea of wanting to establish in America a haven for the outcast of Europe. This would include the debtors from the debtors' prisons in England, the Dissenters and non-Conformist from the Church of England, those Protestants thrown out of the Catholic countries of Europe, and other unfortunate people, good, God-fearing people, but people who had been rejected by their country for one reason or another, whether it be for social, political, economic, or religious reasons. And Colonel Oglethorpe asked if I would serve as Chaplin to the Colony, and I readily agreed! For not only could I be a Chaplain to the Colonists, but I could also be a Missionary to the Indians as well! And so, with great enthusiasm I set sail aboard the ship the "Simmons" along with my brother Charles and Colonel James Oglethorpe, who was returning to America for his second visit to America.

It was a long, hard, tedious voyage. It lasted some one hundred days on the open seas, but while on board, I did have the opportunity to become friends with a group of about twenty-six or so Moravians. Now these Moravians were a religious sect from Germany. They had a vital and healthy relationship with God, and I guess you might say they had a simple piety about them. I recall that once during our voyage, a great storm came upon the sea and all the English-speaking passengers were fearful that all would be lost and all lives taken, and there was great fear and crying and shouting out loud among these English-speaking people. But these Moravians were calm and courageous, they stood on board deck holding hands and singing simple hymns and praises. Somehow, they had a special relationship with God which I did not have, and I envied them greatly. I even attempted to learn German in an effort to converse with them more fully!

Well, we finally arrived in the Colony of Georgia, which by the way was named after King George II of England. The first thing we did was to give thanks to God for our safe journey, and then to pray for our mission. And believe me our mission needed lots of prayers, because for me, it turned out to be a disaster! I can describe it no other way, for me it was a disaster! I had gone to convert the Indians, but the Indians did not care to be converted, at least to my brand of religion. And I had gone to be a Chaplin to the Colonist. You see, I also wanted to establish my disciplines upon the Colonists. At first, they grumbled, then they rebelled. I even heard several of them say that "they would rather spend the rest of their days rotting in a debtors' prison in England, than to be sentenced to the Hell of Wesley's salvation"! So, I fared little better with the Colonist! But we did have some measure of success. We were able to print the first hymnbook in America. This was in Charlestown in 1736. We were also able to establish the first Sunday School in America. This was some fifty years before a Sunday School was established in England and some eighty years before another Sunday School was established in America.

Now my friend George Whitfield who I had mentioned earlier, came to America about this time. He established an orphanage in Bethesda, about fifteen or so miles from Savannah. He moved the Sunday School there to the orphanage, and those of you who are familiar with this area know that this orphanage and this Sunday School are still in existence today, which makes it the longest, continuing operating Sunday School anywhere in the world.

Well, I mentioned that I left America. I must admit that my reasons for leaving America were rather personal. You see when I arrived in America, I met a young, attractive, eighteen-year-old girl by the name of Sophia Hopkey. Miss Hopkey was the niece of the Chief Magistrate here in the Colony. She thought I was handsome and admired my religious fervor. She asked that I tutor her in French and religion. Well, I tutored the young lady, courted her for a period of time. I even considered asking her to marry me. My Moravian friends persuaded me that this was not the thing to do, and I think now rightly so, for shortly thereafter, she promptly turned around and married another young man she had been courting, and this so infuriated me that I refused to allow her to take of Holy Communion or to participate in our church services. And this in turn so infuriated her new husband that he took out charges against me in the courts here in the Colony, even asked that I be tried before a Grand Jury! Well, rather than undergo the embarrassment and humiliation of a public trial, particularly considering the mood of some of the Colonists, I decided to make my way back home to England. So late one night I slipped out of the Colony, made my way on foot to Charlestown, got lost in the swamps for about a day, lived on nothing but a piece of Gingerbread, but I made my way to Charlestown where I preached for seven days, and then set sail back home to England! Well getting back to England I thought I would never get over the embarrassment and humiliation I had suffered here in the Colony. I had gone to convert the Indians, but who was there to convert me? Oh, I know that history looks upon my mission in America as more of a success than I did at the time, but at the time I thought my mission in America was a failure! In fact, I thought my life was a failure! I was almost on the verge of what you might call today a nervous breakdown, and then I met another Moravian by the name of Peter Bohler. Peter Bohler was an evangelistic minister from Germany on his way to America by way of England. Peter Bohler and I became good friends, and I learned a great deal from this, my new Moravian friend! He told me what I needed in my life was faith! He told me that I should preach faith until I found it! He told me that what I needed in my religious life was a vital new spiritual experience and that I should seek this day and night. So that is what I did! Oh, I continued with my prayers, my Bible reading, my fasting and taking of Holy Communion, all those things that I had done in the past, but now, with renewed determination to find that vital new spiritual experience that I had been missing. Then on May 28, 1738, I found that vital new spiritual experience! I remember the day very well! It began as all my days in prayer and Bible reading. And as was my custom, I would arise at 5:00 in the morning, open my Bible at random at a passage, and determine that that passage had some special meaning for me that day! And as I did so on this occasion, I opened my Bible, thrust my finger at random to a passage in the Gospel of St. Mark, and I read these words: "Thou art not far from the Kingdom of God." And having read those words, and thought about them, and having realized that I was not far from the Kingdom of God, I became in a state of spiritual excitement, a state that stayed with me the rest of the day. That afternoon, I attended services at Saint Paul's Cathedral there in London, a beautiful, majestic Cathedral. Perhaps you've been there, or at least seen it on television, it is where Prince Charles and Lady Diana were married a number of years ago. For those of you who are interested in the music ministry of the church, you know, I don't remember the sermon that was preached that day, but I do remember the hymns, particularly the first hymn, and the first stanza of that first hymn. I remember these words, "Out of the depts I cry to you, O Lord, now hear me calling…", as if to say "Hear me O God! Speak to me O God! Tell me of Thy purpose for my life! Tell me of thy plan of salvation!" And I continued in this state of spiritual excitement, although I thought little more about it as I went rather reluctantly that evening to a prayer service being conducted by the Moravians in a little house on Aldersgate Street. And I guess I appeared out of place as I appeared in my priestly garb that evening, and yet I was warmly received, for the Moravians are a warm and friendly people. And although I arrived at dusk, I guess it was a quarter to nine as someone was reading from Martin Luther's Preface to the Epistle of St. Paul to the Romans. And as he was describing how God works in the heart of those who find faith in Christ, I felt my heart strangely warm! I felt I did trust Christ! Christ alone for my salvation! That an assurance was given to me that He had cleansed my sins, even mine, and saved me from a law of sin and death! I knew it was not by my own efforts, not by anything that I could do, but it was through God's mercy through faith in Christ that I could find peace and eternal salvation. Now there was no clapping of hands, no stomping of feet, no shouts of elation there that evening. I know that if a newspaper had been there, they would not have noticed anything of any significance having happened there that evening, and yet, I went forward from there as a changed person, and having experienced personal redemption, I wanted everyone else to experience it as well. And so, at age 35, I went forward from there with a new determination to spread the Good News of salvation by faith wherever and whenever I could, and since I had no parish of my own, the world became my parish!

Now you would think that at 35 years of age, being a son of a Priest of the Church of England, and myself a scholarly, well-educated Priest of the Church of England, with my missionary experience in America and my enthusiasm, that I would be warmly received by the Churches of England. And yet, the contrary was true. And I guess it was because of my enthusiasm, but on many occasions when I tried to preach in the Churches of England, I was refused! On one such occasion as I sought to preach in my father's Church at Epworth, when I was refused the pulpit, I preached instead on my father's tombstone.

Now about that time my friend, George Whitfield, returned to England to raise money for his orphanage, and before he returned to America, he told me that what I needed to do was to preach to the unchurched masses. So, this is what I began to do! I began preaching in the coal mines, in the factories, and in the open fields. I remember once on an April Sunday outside of Bristol, England, I preached to a crowd of some 3,000 people, and this was just the first of many large crowds! After that, I preached to crowds as large as 3, 4, and 5,000, 8, 9, and 10,000 people at a time. Once I even preached to a crowd of some 20.000 people, and all this was at a time when there were no microphones, amplifiers, or PA systems of any kind!

But I was not always warmly received. In fact, on many occasions I was met by mobs! Sticks and stones were thrown at me. On several occasions I was hauled through the streets by my hair - brought before Magistrates on all kind of trumped-up charges! But you know, on almost all of these occasions I was able to preach to the mobs, to the leaders of the mobs and to the Magistrates, and converted many of these people **on the spot**, and allowed to go on my way!

Well, over the next fifty years I guess I preached some 50.000 sermons and travelled some 250,000 miles. Most of that was on horseback, although in my latter years I did travel some by carriage. But you might be interested that as I rode along on horseback reading my Bible, it was not uncommon for me to be so engrossed in my prayer and Bible reading, that I would simply fall off my horse!

Well, throughout this period of time, my emphasis was in three main areas. My first emphasis was in Evangelism, spreading the Gospel and spreading the Good News of Salvation by Faith wherever and whenever I could, and since I had no parish of my own, the world was my parish!

My second emphasis was in organization and administration. Wherever I went I would organize little "Bands", little "Classes", little "Societies", each with its own set of rules. I would appoint lay leaders and lay ministers and call them together annually in an annual conference, much as your lay leaders and ministers are called together in an annual conference today.

My third emphasis was in the printed page. I wrote a great number of treatises on the Old and New Testament. I wrote a great number of hymns. My brother, Charles, wrote over 6.000 hymns including, "Hark the Herald Angels Sing," "O For a Thousand Tongues to Sing My Great Redeemer's Praise," and many more, many of which you would recognize. But you know, my most popular publication was not a religious publication at all, but a book on household cures. It was so popular that it underwent edition, after edition, after edition - earned a great deal of money which we poured back into the other Methodist publications and the Methodist's Societies. Have you ever heard the expression that, "Cleanliness is next to Godliness," and wondered where that came from? Well, that was in my book of household cures!

Well, throughout this period of time, Methodism grew like wildfire! It spread from England on into Ireland, and from Ireland on into America. Very early two lay ministers that I had appointed in Ireland went to America, one went to Baltimore, one to New York! And Methodism began to spread in America as well! Slowly at first. But I guess I was 65 years of age when I first heard the cries for help from America. At one of these annual conferences, one of these conferences assembled, I said, "Our brothers in America are crying out loudly for help," and I asked, "Who will go and help them?" And I received five offers to go to America, and I sent three, including Francis Asbury. Now Francis Asbury had been a blacksmith in England and went to America to become the great leader of Methodism in America, himself travelling some 275,000 miles throughout America on horseback preaching the Good News of Salvation by Faith and spreading Methodism. But when the American Revolution broke out, Methodism became under suspicion, because of its association with the Church of England, and its association with the Crown.

In an effort to help the situation, I wrote a pamphlet which I entitled, "A Calm Address to The American Colonies," and in this "Calm Address to The American Colonies", not only did I urge "calm," but I also urged the Colonist to support the English King! Now this did not have the calming effect that I had hoped it would have upon America. But despite this, by the end of the American Revolution, there were still some 15,000 Methodist in America and some 80 or so lay ministers. And Methodism continued to spread here in America because it was a natural for America! You see, with the itinerant system, we did not wait for people to come to us, we went out to them. By this means we were able to go to the scattered villages and farms. We were able to follow the "Westward Movement" as it moved West, all the time preaching the Gospel, spreading the Good News of Salvation by Faith, and spreading Methodism!

But we continued to hear the cries for help from America, for you see, we never intended to form a new Church in America, only so many Societies. We always intended that the sacraments would be administered by ordained ministers, so there was always a sore need for ordained ministers in America. And when I told this to the Bishop of London and when he turned his back on me and refused to help, I knew it was up to me to act, so I took it upon myself to appointed Thomas Coke to go to America to be my Superintendent, or Bishop, if you please. Now I was highly criticized for what was called this "usurpation of authority!" In fact, my brother, Charles, was among my chief critics! He even wrote a hymn. If I recall the words correctly, they went something like this: "How easily are Bishops made, at men's and women's whim, Wesley his hands on Coke hath laid, but who laid their hand on him?" Well fortunately, this was not one of Charles more popular hymns! Thomas Coke did go to America. He took with him a letter asking that Francis Asbury serve as Co-Bishop. When they arrived, they decided to hold an election for this purpose, so a call went out to some eighty or so persons. Some 60 or so braved the cold New England weather to arrive at the Lovely Lane Chapel there in Baltimore, Maryland on December 24, 1784. And when that "Christmas Conference" had ended several days later, great thing had been accomplished: twelve ministers had been ordained, Francis Asbury and Thomas Coke had been elected as Bishops and were ordained, and most importantly, the Methodist Church was formerly established as an independent church here in America! And this my dear friends was the formal beginning of the Methodist Church in America!

Looking back over the years, I am proud of the role that I played in this great Methodist movement! I think I did that which God had called on me to do! I think this was the purpose for which God had spared me from the fire so many years before, and I'm proud now to be called, "The Father of Methodism"! And it was a great pleasure being here with you today, as, "John Wesley"!

Figure 1. Don Germano's first portrayal in 1984, the next 4 are from his most recent portrayal at his son's church in January 2023.

Figure 2. Don Germano portraying John Wesley with his son, The Rev. Dr. Brian Germano" (January 2023).

POEMS OF FAITH

The Biblical poems that I have included herein and that follow, were mostly written to accompany lessons I was teaching in Sunday School. The other poems I have included were some I included in a gathering of poems and devotionals I gave to my wife on our 60th wedding anniversary.

THE CREATION UPDATED

Genesis 1 & 2

In the First Book of Moses called Genesis,
We read that God Created the heaven and the earth.
But in the beginning the earth was void,
And without form or color and was of little worth.

When God saw the darkness
He decided to create light,
And seeing that it was good,
He separated day from night.

Then God created the land and the seas
And saw that they too were good.
Then brought forth grass and herbs and trees,
Fruit trees, pines, oaks, and dogwood.

For the waters and the seas,
God created fish of every kind.
And for the air, winged fowl,
And all the birds he could find.

Then for the land, God brought forth,
Living creatures of every kind,
Cattle and sheep, horses, and pigs,
And everything else that was on His mind.

And all this was good,
But still looked mighty bland,
For although there was light,
There was no color upon the land.

There was no yellow, red, or white,
There was no purple or even blue.
There was no orange, gold, or silver,
Nor was there green of any hue.

So God decided to order up some colors,
To brighten up the earth He had made.
But then He realized there was a problem,
So His plans might be delayed.

For 'tho He could go on the internet,
And order all the colors He might need,
Who was there to drive the UPS truck,
To deliver the colors He decreed?

So God created man,
To make the delivery.
And man delivered all the colors,
That you and I now can see.

And for his service, God gave man,
Dominion over all the earth,
Over the fowl in the air and the fish in the sea,
The cattle, and everything else of worth.

Then God gave man a woman
To love and be his mate,
To live together upon the earth,
A world to cherish and to celebrate.

Now God has made all these things,
All that He thought He should.
He looked at all that He had made,
And behold, it was very good!

So having created heaven and earth,
And all that dwells therein,
On the seventh day God rested,
And said, "Let the world begin!"

NICODEMUS

John 2: 13-19; 3: 1-16; 7: 50-52; 19: 38-42

My name is Nicodemus.
I am sure you've heard of me,
For I am a devout religious leader of the Jews,
A teacher of Israel, and a Pharisee.

I, of course, live in Jerusalem,
The only place to be,
A place of learning
And of high religious morality.

But here of late a man named Jesus,
 Has come to this holy town,
Talking about building up in three days
The Temple after tearing it down.

Yet here at Passover
Many believe in his name,
When they saw what he did,
'Tho our leaders are sorry he came.

As for me, I do not know what to think!
A lot I don't understand!
How could he do and say the things he does,
For he is just a man?

Perhaps if I could go to him,
And speak to him at night,
For I dare not go during the day
My colleagues would not think it right!

So, I go in the cover of darkness,
To speak with this curious man,
With hope that his answers will clear my mind
I really think they can.

And when we meet, I say, "Rabbi,"
I know that God is there with you,
For man alone cannot perform
The miracles that you do!"

But Jesus's response is a curiosity,
As he answers and says to me,
"Except a man be born again,
The Kingdom of God he will never see!"

"But how can a man be born again,
To enter his mother's womb?"
This makes no sense, I do not understand,
Then Jesus begins to resume.

And now he talks of being born of the spirit,
Which still makes no sense to me.
I'm afraid I still don't "get it!"
How could these things be?

So, I leave that night still confused,
With questions on my mind.
But the more I see and hear of Jesus,
In him I come to believe in time.

And now my colleagues would condemn this man,
'Tho for reasons they had none.
But I tell them, "Does our law not judge a man,
Before it hears him and knows what he has done?"

But then I learn he's been condemned
And upon a cross he dies,
Without a lawful hearing
And testimony based on lies!

So, my friend and I are given leave,
To take the body down,
And I bring myrrh and aloe to anoint the body,
Before he's to be bound.

Now I learn he's risen from the dead,
And has spoken to many he's known.
And 'tho there is still much I don't understand,
I think in faith I've grown.

I now can say I do believe,
Although I still think it odd,
But I do know Jesus is the Christ,
And that he came from God!

THE WOMAN AT THE WELL

John 4:1-42

I lived in a town in Samaria,
 Where Jacob had a well.
My life had not been happy,
And I have a lot I could tell.

I have had no meaningful relationships,
'Tho I have lived with five different men,
And living with another now,
Which others call a sin.

So I carry this burden of loneliness,
And guilt as I live each day,
But go about my daily life,
No matter what people say.

But one of these days I go to the well,
To draw the water I need.
A simple task I've done many times,
A necessary daily deed.

And it is always uneventful.
No one is usually there.
And only women come sometimes,
But even they don't care.

They have their own burdens,
As I have mine.
They know my reputation,
So they are never very kind.

But something was different,
As I came to draw water one day,
A man was there sitting by the well,
Appearing very tired, having come a very long way.

I was surprised for a man to speak to me,
And in so friendly and pleasant way.
As he simply asked for something to drink
I hardly knew what to say.

Although he was a man and I a woman,
And he a Jew and I not of his kind,
And I a Samaritan looked down upon by Jewish men,
This man didn't seem to mind.

But I still wondered and asked,
"How is it that you a Jewish man ask me,
A Samaritan woman for a drink?"
But then he talked of "Living Water" from God
And I didn't know what to think.

He said this "Living Water" from God
Would never run out!
Which I thought would be nice to have.
But then he changed the subject of what we were talking about.

And he told me to call my husband,
But when I said I had none,
 He said "true, you've had five,
And the man you're living with now, he's not one!"

I thought this man a prophet,
Because of all he did see.
And when I told him I knew the "Messiah" was coming,
He said, **"I am he!"**

As the man was joined by his friends,
I remained astonished by all that he did say,
And I ran to tell all the people I knew,
Of this man I had met that day!

Could this be the Christ,
This man who had told me all I had ever done?
I think my life will never be the same,
For I have met Christ, the "Messiah" – **HE IS THE ONE!**

NOTE:

John 4:39 *And many of the Samaritans of that city believed on him for the sayings of the woman which testified, "He told me all that I had ever did."*

According to the theologian, Barbara Brown Taylor, this conversation of Jesus with the woman at the well is the longest recorded conversation of Jesus with anyone in the Bible, including his disciples, members of his family, or his accusers. She is one of the few persons in the Gospels to whom Jesus revealed his identity. And perhaps most importantly, "… she is the first person in John's gospel to straightway become an evangelist and bring an entire city to a saving knowledge of Jesus." (Debbie Thomas, **Journey with Jesus, The Woman at the Well)**

A LIFE CHANGING DAY

Mark 2: 1-12

(The story of Jesus healing the paralytic lowered through the roof)

From birth I could not walk
So life was not easy for me.
Some folks looked the other way,
And pretended that they just didn't see.

Others pitied me,
But did not know what to say.
A simple "hello" would have been enough,
Or "I hope you have a good day!"

So now I lay on my mat,
With a crutch down by my leg,
And as strangers come by,
I beg!

It is enough to simply get by,
As I lie there day by day.
With little hope for things to change,
Accepting "come what may!"

But I have four friends,
I've made along the way,
Who will stop by and say, "hello",
And talk to me almost every day.

They are caring soles who understand,
That I am just like they:
I am a man who has a mind,
Can think and hear what people say.

These friends don't pity me,
But truly care,
About my life
And the burdens that I bear.

And where I live in Capernaum,
We all hear of a man one day,
And of the miracles he performs
And of what he has to say.

That he talks of love and of God,
And heals the sick, the blind, and the lame,
And tells us to love our neighbors,
And "Jesus" is his name.

So, my friends and I
We talk of this man,
And we have faith that one day for me,
This Jesus will do what he can!

But the crowds are large,
And he is inside,
To reach this Jesus there is no way,
Even if the doors were wide.

So, my friend have a plan and they climb on the roof,
Where this Jesus is preaching that day,
And with me on my mat, they lower me down,
Not knowing what Jesus might say.

But Jesus had compassion,
And the words that he did say,
Was to take up my mat and go home,
So I picked up my mat and went away!

And as I look back on that wonderful day,
I thank Jesus and God and my four friends too,
For giving me new life,
And for all that I can now do!

BARTIMAEUS

Mark 10: 46-52

I saw a man sitting by the road,
He didn't look like me,
And he had a sign that read, "Please Help!"
Then I saw that he couldn't see!

My first thought was to walk on by,
For I had a lot to do,
And a lot of other people needed help,
I could think of quite a few.

But then I thought of a story I had read
In the Gospel of Mark and what it had to say
About another blind man named "Bartimaeus"
Who encountered Jesus on the Jericho Road one day.

And having heard of Jesus
And what he had heard Jesus could do
Of healing the sick and the lame,
And even the blind made to see too,

The beggar cried out,
"Jesus, Son of David, have mercy on me!"
But the crowd tried to quiet him down,
And told him to let Jesus be.

But the beggar cried out even louder,
"Son of David, have mercy on me!"
"And what do you want me to do for you? "Jesus asked.
"Restore my sight that I might see!"

"Your faith has made you well!"
Jesus told him as the beggar came his way.
And his sight was restored,
And he rejoiced and followed Jesus out of Jericho that very day.

Now although **my** beggar knew not my name,
And did not shout out to me,
His sign spoke volumes of his need,
So, I stopped to share and show him mercy.

I remember well what Jesus said,
To his disciples on another day,
To "love your neighbor as yourself",
And to show mercy to all in need who come your way!
(Mark 12: 31)

ZACCHAEUS

Luke 19: 1-10

"The Gospel of the Outcast"

"Zacchaeus was a little man,
A wee little man was he!"
I always liked this image,
Of a "Tax Man" up a tree!

On his way to Jerusalem
Jesus came to Jericho,
Now a thriving city of Joshua fame,
With twenty miles yet to go!

Zacchaeus lived in this crossroad town,
Collecting taxes from his fellow Jews.
A notable visitor was coming his way,
And Zacchaeus heard this exciting news!

To get a look he climbed a tree,
And Jesus spotted him there that day.
He said, "Zacchaeus, come on down,
I must stay at your house if I may!"

So, Zacchaeus came on down,
And welcomed this man with dinner,
While the people murmured, quite disturbed,
"This man, he dines with a sinner!"

"The Son of Man came to seek and save,
those who are lost!" Jesus said!
And Zacchaeus had climbed a tree that day,
For that's where the Spirit had led!

So, after meeting this man named Jesus,
Zacchaeus, himself, became a new man!
"I'll give half I have to the poor, he said,
And to the cheated, four times when I can!"

So, on His way to Jerusalem
Where Jesus will lose **His** life,
Jesus stopped and dined with a tax collector,
And brought **him** "salvation" and a new life!

THE TOMB

Matthew 28: 1-10; Mark 16: 1-7
Luke 24: 1-12; John 20: 1-18

They took Him down from the cross
And laid Him in the tomb that day!
Then placed a stone at its end,
And then they went away.

All this they did in such great haste,
Because the sabbath was near,
And they would return with spices to anoint,
This one they loved so dear.

So, on Sunday morn the women would return,
To do what must be done.
And 'tho they didn't know it then,
The victory had been won.

So, as they came to the tomb,
On their minds that sad day,
Was how that stone so very large,
Could be rolled away.

But to their surprise it had been done,
The stone had been rolled away,
And 'tho the Lord was not inside,
A man in white there began to say:

"Why seek thee the living among the dead?"
And this angel continued to say,
To meet in Galilee,
For Jesus had risen that very day!

Then Peter ran to the tomb
Just for himself to see.
But found only the linen cloth,
Neatly folded and very orderly.

Mary Magdalen also came,
And was the first to see,
And knew at once it was her Lord,
When Jesus simply said - **"Mary!"**

So now we all know the risen Lord,
And now we can see clearly,
When Jesus rose from death that day
He had won the victory!

FRANCIS OF ASSISI

I was born of a noble family,
In an Italian town called Assisi.
As a youth I was rather wild and pretentious
With grandiose ideas of what I wanted to be.

I wanted to be a knight,
With shiny armor and doing great deeds.
I had everything I wanted,
And cared little about my needs.

My father was a silk merchant,
Selling cloth of every kind.
He wanted me to help in the business,
But that was furthest from my mind.

I persuaded him to buy me armor,
So I could become a knight,
And with a fine horse and sword,
I left for Perugia to join in the fight.

But our battle was not successful,
As goes the fate of war,
And I was taken prisoner,
Along with many more.

In chains I spent a year,
Until at last peace came,
And I was ransomed and came back home,
"Tho I was not the same.

In prison I had shared my food,
And learned humility!
But still had no interest in my father's business,
And did not know what I wanted to be.

I tried again to be a knight,
And persuaded my father to outfit me once more,
But I sold my armor, sword, and horse,
And gave the proceeds to the poor.

Like the Prodigal Son I returned back home
Because I had heard the voice of God,
But he did not tell me what to do there,
And I thought it rather odd!

My father now in a rage,
Publicly denounced this his oldest son,
So, I stripped naked before the town,
And said, "Of worldly things I wanted none!"

All I had I gave away,
And I lived on charity,
And waited on the voice of God,
To tell me what He wanted me to be.

At some point I heard that voice,
"Rebuild my church!" I heard Him say.
So, I began to rebuild the Chapel of St. Damiana
With help who came my way.

I became a penitent and a beggar.
I nursed and lived with lepers,
And restored other ruined chapels,
Including that of St. Mary of the Angels.

I lived a simple life,
Preaching peace and brotherly love,
And always listening very intently
For the voice from above.

Others began to follow,
And soon eleven came my way,
To live a simple life,
And hear what I had to say!

So, I composed some simple rules,
And set out for Rome one day,
To ask the Pope to bless us,
And to our Order give his OK!

Our rules were very simple,
To follow and live like Jesus,
To follow in His footsteps,
So that God would love and bless us!

Now a young Noblewoman
By the name of Clair of Assisi
Came to join our Order one day,
To live and be like me.

So the "Order of Poor Clair" was founded,
And other women joined her too,
To live a life of poverty
And do as Jesus would do.

The "Franciscans" now had many followers,
And we went out two by two,
To preach the Gospel, and the life of devotion and poverty
To all the countries we went to!

I believed that nature was the mirror of God,
There was Brother Sun, Wind, and Fire, and Sister Moon,
I loved and respected them all,
And stories of my love rose up soon!

I wrote poems and canticles,
And then stories about me began to circulate too!
Some were fanciful!
Some were true!

One: In the town of Gubbio in Italy,
A wolf terrorized the town!
I met with the wolf and with it made peace,
So the town would feed the wolf and it could come around!

Two: On a mission trip I stopped to pray
To a group of birds one day.
They gathered around me and would not leave,
And would not fly away!

So, I lived my life like Jesus,
And did what God told me to do!
I had followed the teachings of Jesus,
And founded some religious orders that were brand new!

NOTE:

A few facts concerning Francis of Assisi*

In 1223 St. Francis arranged for the first nativity scene.

1n 1224, he received the "Stigmata", the wounds of Jesus in his hands, feet, and side. He was the first person in Christian tradition to bear the wounds of Christ's Passion.

He died during the evening hours of October 3, 1226, at the age of forty-four, while listening to a reading he had requested of Psalms 142.

Two years later, Pope Gregory IX canonized him, naming him officially, "Saint Francis." The next day the Pope laid the foundation stone for the Basilica of St. Francis, where St. Francis was buried two years later.

Along with Catherine of Sienna, St. Francis is designated "Patron Saint of Italy."

St. Francis was a great lover of animals and ecology and was also declared the "Patron Saint of Animals", and in 1979 "Patron Saint of the Ecology" by Pope John Paul.

In 2013, upon his election as Pope, Archbishop and Cardinal Bergoglio chose the name, "Pope Francis", in honor of St. Francis, the first to take that name.

The Franciscan Order which St. Francis founded, is the largest monastic order in the Catholic Church.

St. Francis is considered by many to be the first Italian poet. The poem, "Make Me an Instrument of Your Peace" is attributed to him, although there is no proof of his authorship.

St. Francis is one of the most venerated religious figures in Christianity!

*From Wikipedia and Encyclopedia Britannia

THERE ARE NO TEARS IN HEAVEN

Luke 23: 40-43; John 14: 2-3; Psalms 23;
1 Cor. 13: 12

There are no tears in heaven!
This I believe is true!
But the streets may not be paved with gold!
I really wish I knew!

When Jesus was dying on the cross,
He told the thief that day,
"Today you'll be in paradise!"
And I believe what he did say!

I believe that Jesus,
And those who have gone before,
Will greet me that blessed day,
And welcome me at heaven's door!

Then Jesus will show me the place,
He has prepared there just for me,
Those rooms he talked about with his disciples,
A place so heavenly!

I'll probably hear the heavenly choir,
And perhaps can join it too!
Family and friends will all be there,
Lots of folks I knew!

And pain and suffering
Will be no more!
Only green pastures and still waters,
With peace and no more war!

'Tho now I only see in part,
And only thru glass darkly,
I think in heaven all will be made known,
And I will then see clearly!

So, I look forward to being with my Lord,
And being with Jesus to whom I prayed!
To be in a place where there are no tears,
The Heavenly Kingdom He made!

WHO NEEDS ROOM?

Our Preacher[1] once told us,
That "the devil don't need much room!"
And I guess it's true,
'Cause our Preacher is wise and intelligent too!

Then our Preacher went on to tell us
What a person must do,
To keep the devil away
From me and you!

But I guess the devil is also wise.
And is intelligent too,
And probably would like to win
For himself, a soul or two!

So, we must be vigilant,
And to our faith be true,
Cause Christians "don't need much room" either,
To do what they must do!

---

[1] Pastor Randy Lucas, Highlands United Methodist Church, Highlands, North Carolina

STOWAWAY VOICE

My Pastor[2] speaks of a "Stowaway Voice,"
That speaks inside his head,
And tries to keep him on the "right path,"
But sometimes he would rather just be himself instead!

In a recent sermon he said that voice
Sometimes speaks to his heart when it comes around,
And says, "You are the salt and light of the world,
And are standing on Holy Ground!"
(Matthew 5: 13-16)

I think I know that same "Stowaway Voice,"
That tags along every day.
Sometimes I think it keeps me "straight,"
To do right and watch what I might say.

But there is another "Stowaway Voice,"
That sometimes says, "My son, …,"
(It's of a more sinister and less friendly voice)
That says, "go ahead and do it, it's fun!"

But I try to listen to only the "Good Voice",
Because I know it's for my own good,
And it keeps me on the "straight and narrow",
And doing and saying only what I should!

---

[2] Pastor Randy Lucas, Highlands United Methodist Church, Highlands, North Carolina

SILENCE

A few days ago
I ordered online,
A box of "Silence",
Advertised as "One of a kind!"

By UPS
It arrived today,
So, I quickly opened the box,
And read what the instructions had to say.

It cautioned not to use it,
If you had something wise or worthwhile to say,
But suggested it would always be advisable,
To use a little each and every day.

And it would be better,
To use at times and be thought about,
Than to speak about what is on your mind
And be proved a fool without a doubt![3]

So, I think I will use it,
To meditate,
And listen for the word of God,
And before I speak, just hesitate!

I'll use a little to give away,
To some folks who talk a lot,
Who won't let you get a word in edgewise,
And by the time you can, you forgot!

Anyway, I guess it's good to leave unsaid,
Much that is on your mind,
Words that anger or upset someone,
That may be hurtful or unkind!

---

[3] A variation by Abraham Lincoln / and or Mark Twain

"Silence is Golden," [4]
Or so I have heard,
So sometimes its better just to remain silent,
And never say a word!

I'll end with what my Pastor[5] has to say,
"That it is in the silence,
That sometimes life's deeper truths can just be easier to bear...!"
And in silence, to know God's presence!

[4] Thomas Carlyle
[5] Pastor Randy Lucas, Highlands United Methodist Church, Highlands, North Carolina

A SPECIAL ORDER

(Self–Control)

I saw an ad on TV today,
For a box of "Self-Control."
They said it was good for the body,
And also, it was good for the soul.

A bargain at 19.95, (plus shipping and handling),
(And a free gift if I ordered today!)
So, I placed my order, and got an email,
That my shipment was on its way!

Upon receipt, the instructions said,
I should use a little each day,
To help me learn to be careful,
Of what I might do or say!

It also suggested its use,
To meet everyone's goal,
Of bringing one's emotions
Under one's control.

A few buyers' comments,
 Were also there to read,
Which rated the product highly,
And told what one might need.

One said its use each day,
Would also help,
In keeping one's thoughts and emotions
 To oneself!

So, I'll use this product,
And use it every day,
Be patient, avert anger,

And watch what I do and say!
I'll try not to make foolish decisions,
Based on impulse feelings,
But follow the teachings of Jesus,
In all my actions and my dealings!

The "Fruits of the Spirit"
As Paul wrote of in Galatians, Chapter Five,
I think are the results of this "Self–Control",
To which we must all daily strive!

Oh yes, the free gift,
 I'm sure you would like to know,
A bookmark with Count Leo Tolstoy's quote:
"There never has been, and cannot be,
 a good life without self-control!"

THE NOVICE AND THE ABBOT

(Anonymous Story)

I once heard the story,
Of a young man one day
Who joined a Monastic Order,
That limited what one could say!

The Abbot told the Novice,
That he could only speak aloud
Two words every five years,
That's all that was allowed!

So, after five years
The Novice came to the Abbot and said,
"Bed hard!"
For that was where he laid his head.

Ten years now passed.
And now a little older and looking rather sad,
The now Brother Monk came again to the Abbot,
And said his two words, "Food bad!"

Another five years
And now getting rather old,
He approached the Abbot again,
And said, "Room cold!"

Twenty years now had passed,
And Brother Monk was now ready to "split",
And came to the Abbot,
Simply saying, "I quit!"

The Abbot was not surprised,
And said, My Brother, you are not to blame,
For you have done nothing but complain,
Since the day that you first came!"

THE CHRISTMAS PARADE

On December 3rd of '22
Highlands held its Christmas Parade
With cars and floats and three marching bands,
And colorful costumes, many were homemade.

And Bagpipes led the big parade,
Played by our own Margaret and by Glenn.
And many said that this parade,
Was the best it had ever been.

Our Church[6] was a part of this parade,
With a large banner that led!
"Wise Men still seek Him!"
Is what the banner said.

Mary and Joseph came behind,
With Mary riding on a donkey.
And soon the baby Jesus will come,
Completing the Holy Family!

Then came three camels,
And three Wisemen too.
All knew their parts,
And knew what to do!

So HUMC[7] played its part,
Of this there was no doubt!
We showed the people of Highlands,
What Christmas was all about!

---

[6] Highlands United Methodist Church, Highlands, North Carolina
[7] Highlands United Methodist Church, Highlands, North Carolina

THE NIGHT SKY, DECEMBER 14, 2021

"In the beginning
God created the heavens and the earth!"
What a wonderful world He created
And to which He gave birth!

This morning, quite early and still dark,
I looked up at the night sky.
I was looking for a meteorite shower,
That I had read about, visible to the naked eye.

Dots of light, some dim, some bright,
Some twinkling, poked their way through the darkness,
And I gazed in wonder and in awe,
At God's great creation in that moment of stillness.

Although the meteorite shower
 I did not see,
The night sky with its twinkling lights
Was quite enough for me!

But then, in the corner of my eye,
A glimpse of a falling star came into sight,
And I marveled at this wonderful event,
God had created for the night!

THE LAWYER

Luke 10: 25-37

The Story of the Good Samaritan

I was a lawyer,
Many years ago.
I was well educated.
There wasn't much I didn't know!

As for my background,
I was a Jew.
I knew right from wrong,
And always knew what to do!

In Capernaum where I lived,
There was this man of late,
Who performed "so-called" miracles,
And taught of love, not hate.

And I, an expert in religious law,
Stood up before the rest,
To challenge this man called Jesus,
And put his teachings to the test.

So I asked this teacher,
Aside from refraining from conflict and strife,
"What must a man do,
To inherit eternal life?"

But rather than answer
He asked me that day,
"What is written in the Law?
What do you have to say?

The answer was kosher.
I knew it myself:
"Love the Lord your God with all your heart,
And your neighbor as yourself."

But I pressed him further,
For I had some doubt,
"Who is this neighbor", I said,
"That we are talking about?"

And then Jesus told this story,
Of a traveler on a road to Jericho,
Who was attacked by robbers,
Hurt and dying, and there they left him so.

Now two holy men
Walked on by,
And left the injured man,
There to die!

You see, the Priest and this Levite religious man,
Didn't want to get involved,
Or get ritually contaminated.
This was not their problem to resolve!

But a Samaritan man happened on by,
And had compassion on this dying man,
And bandaged his wounds,
And said, "I'll do what I can!"

So he took him to an inn,
And paid there for his care,
And asked the innkeeper,
To look after his welfare,

And said when he returned,
He would pay all that was due,
For taking care of the injured man,
And for all that might accrue.

"Now which was the neighbor?"
Jesus asked of me –
And I quickly replied,
"The one who showed mercy!"

And so, I learned a lesson that day,
From the story that Jesus told,
Of the one who showed compassion and mercy
To the man on the Jericho Road.

MY STORY

Luke 15: 3-32

The Story of the Lost Sheep, Coin, and the Prodigal Son

Jesus tells three stories,
Of how God and the angles rejoice
Over one soul repenting and returning to God,
With heart and mind and voice!

The first of these stories
Tells of a single lost sheep that goes astray,
And the shepherd leaves his flock in search,
Until the lost sheep has returned that day.

The second tells of a poor widow woman,
Who has lost her only "mite,"
And rejoices with all her friends,
When after searching, she finds it later that night.

The third story is my very own!
Of two boys, and I the youngest son,
Who wants my inheritance **now,**
So I can go out and have some fun!

So I ask my father,
Contrary to the rules of the day.
But my father has a big heart,
Grants my wish, with very little to say.

So I leave my home,
To go to a "better" land,
Th raise "hell "and enjoy life,
And have all the fun that I can!

And there I spend all my money,
In sin and riotous living,
Without a second thought
Of prayer or even thanksgiving.

Then destitute and all alone,
A famine comes across the land.
So I search in vain to find a job and a friend,
But no one lends a hand.

I finally find a job,
Feeding pigs, but having no food of my own,
Then finally come to my senses,
For even servants have plenty of food back home.

I could return to my father,
And beg that he forgive me,
And let me be a servant,
For that's all I'm worthy to be.

But my father isn't pouting,
He sees me from far away,
And rushes out to meet me,
And embraces me in a loving way!

He puts a robe upon my back,
A ring and sandals he gives me too.
The fatted calf he orders killed.
To celebrate, there is nothing he will not do.

Now my older brother was unhappy,
With the celebration of my return,
For he had always been faithful,
Yet for him, there seemed no concern.

But I "…was lost and now am found,"
My father said in joy!
"My son was dead but is alive again.
Thank God for the return of my boy!"

Sometimes we children make stupid choices,
That hurt ourselves and others too.
But our father still loves us,
No matter what we do!

Now Jesus sees us all,
The faithful and the sinners that roam,
As children of God, all of whom He loves,
And always welcomes them back home!

NOTE:

In our story, the father represents God, the rebellious son represents those spiritually lost, and the older brother the Jewish leaders who resents Jesus associating with "sinners."

WHERE JESUS WALKED

"O Little town of Bethlehem"
Who knew what you would be?
For here the baby Jesus was born,
The Savior for you and for me!
(Luke 2:4, Matthew 2:1)

For thirty years
Nazareth is Jesus's home.
He lives there as a carpenter,
And seldom does he roam.
(Matthew 2:23, Luke 2:39)

"What good can come out from Nazareth?"
Their world does not know what can!
But here, Jesus grew in body, mind, and spirit,
And in favor of God and man!
(John 1:46)

In the Synagogue there in Nazareth, Jesus began to preach,
And thought he'd be respected,
But learned in one's hometown,
One cannot be accepted.
(Luke 4: 116-30)

When John the Baptist was imprisoned,
 Jesus left for Galilee,
And there called some Disciples,
By the Galilean Sea.
(Matthew 4: 12, 18-21)

At a wedding in Cana,
Jesus turns water into wine!
This was the first miracle of Jesus,
And in John's Gospel, the very first "sign!"
(John 2: 1-11)

Around the town of Capernaum
Jesus centers his ministry.
He heals the sick, the blind, and the lame,
For all the world to see!

In Samaria there is a well
Where a woman comes one day,
And she is astonished and believes,
Because of all that Jesus will say!
(John 4:4-42)

Bethsaida was a small town,
Where the Jorden River flowed to the Galilean Sea.
And it was here that Jesus,
Healed a blind man and gave him sight to see!
(Mark 8: 22-25)

Bethsaida was the birthplace,
Of Phillip, Simon Peter, and Andrew.
And near here Jesus fed the 5,000,
And walked on water too!
(John 1: 44, Luke 9: 10-17, Mark 6: 45-52)

As Jesus approached Jericho one day,
To Him a blind beggar shouted out,
"Jesus, Son of David, have mercy on me!"
And Jesus turned about.

Then Jesus asked the beggar,
"What do you want of me?"
"Restore my sight" the beggar said.
 And Jesus said, "Your faith has let you see!"
(Luke 18:35-43)

In Jerusalem, Jesus heals a paralytic,
By the Pool of Bethesda there,
'Tho the healing was on the Sabbath,
Jesus really didn't care!
(John 5: 1-9)

On the slopes of the Mount of Olives,
Near Jerusalem, is the town of Bethany,
The town of Mary, Martha and Lazarus,
There Lazarus is raised by Jesus, for all the world to see!
(John 11: 1-44)

There on a cross in Jerusalem
Jesus will die one sad day for our sin,
But three days later will rise alive,
For the souls of Man to win!

On the Road to Emmaus, Jesus walked one day,
With Cleopas and another, who did not recognize him 'till night,
When dining together their eyes were opened,
Then Jesus disappeared from sight!
(Luke 24: 13-35)

To the vicinity of Bethany,
With His Disciples, Jesus led the eleven.
Lifting up his hands He blessed them,
Then ascended into Heaven.
(Luke 24: 50-53)

These are just some of the towns,
Where Jesus walked and knew,
That changed the world forever more,
And made it better for me and you!

CAPERNAUM

I am the town of Capernaum,
First established the 2nd Century BC,
A fishing village on the Sea of Galilee.
For a visit, come along with me!

I was there in Biblical times,
And known in New Testament fame.
Matthew, Mark, Luke and John,
All mention me by name.

I was the hometown,
Of some folks you might know,
Of Matthew, Simon Peter, Andrew, James and John,
A town with lots of "soul!"

Upon hearing of the arrest of John the Baptist,
From Nazareth to Capernaum Jesus came.
Here He taught and did those "signs",
That soon won Jesus fame!
(Matthew 4: 12-13)

Jesus came to live with me.
Capernaum was a favorite place.
And Jesus did a lot of good here,
He used it as his base!

It was near my town of Capernaum,
That the ministry of Jesus will begin
By the calling of four disciples,
A ministry that will never end!
(Mark 1: 16-20)

Jesus spent much time in Capernaum,
Teaching and healing here!
As the center of His ministry,
 Jesus words spread far and near.

Simon Peter had a house here,
His mother-in-law was ill.
Jesus healed her and made her well,
God gave his Son the skill!
(Luke4: 38-39)

Does your teacher pay the Temple Tax?
Of Simon Peter the authorities here wanted to see.
"Catch a fish with a coin in its mouth", said Jesus,
"And with it pay the Tax for you and me!"
(Matthew 17: 24-27)

Here in Capernaum you might meet Matthew,
A tax collector for Rome.
Here Matthew came to follow Jesus,
And here he had a home.
(Matthew 9: 9; Mark 2: 13-14; Luke 5; 27-28)

There was a Synagogue here,
Where Jesus came and taught,
And all were astonished by His teachings,
Giving them much food for thought.
(Mark 1: 21-22)

Here Jesus said, "I am the bread of life,
And down from Heaven I came!"
Eternal life shall be yours,"
If you feed on this bread in my name!"
(John 6: 48, 58-59)

There was a man with an unclean spirit,
Here at the Synagogue one day,
And Jesus said, "Come out of him!"
And the unclean spirit "spirited" away!
(MARK 1: 21-28)

Here a paralyzed man
Through the roof was lowered down,
And Jesus cured and forgave his sins,
And all were amazed who gathered 'round!
(Mark 2: 1-12)

A Roman Centurion had a paralyzed servant,
And with faith came to Jesus here one day.
"No need to go, just say the word,
And he'll be cured with just the words you say!"

To Jesus such faith He had not seen,
 And He said, "Go! Let it be done!",
And the servant in Cana was healed that day,
By just the words of God's only Son!
(Luke 7: 1-10)

So don't forget my little town,
For much has happened here.
I am the proud little town of Capernaum,
My fame has travelled far and near!

THE YOUNGEST MAGI

Matthew 2: 1-12

I lived in the East.
I studied the sky at night,
The movement of the stars,
Looking for each wonderous sight!

My colleagues and I were well respected,
And well educated too!
Studying the heavens we looked for "signs",
That might tell us what to do!

As my colleagues and I gathered 'round,
Looking up at the sky one night,
We saw a brand-new star rising there,
That was shining very bright!

It meant to us a child was to be born,
Of royal and divine birth,
So we went to Jerusalem to further inquire,
The birthplace of this great child of worth!

There we asked where this child was to be born,
That we now heard was to be King of the Jews.
And King Herod there had called his Chief Priest and Scribes
To help discern to him this "disturbing news"!

The Prophets had said, "in Bethlehem",
They told the King that day,
And he told us to go and find that child,
And report back to him that same way!

So we followed the star to Bethlehem,
Where at a house that star shone brightly 'round,
And there we saw mother and child,
And giving homage, we knelt down!

There we presented gifts of gold, frankincense, and myrrh,
Then returned home another way,
Having heard in a dream to Herod not go,
For what he might do or say!

Thirty or so years had now passed,
And I thought of that trip long ago,
When we saw that blessed child in Bethlehem,
Where he is now, I'd really like to know!

So again, now alone, I set out for Bethlehem,
To try this blessed child to find
His whereabouts, and what has happened to him,
All still weighing heavenly on my mind!

There, I learned he was raised in Nazareth,
And then became a Rabbi and Teacher of Men.
He travelled throughout Judea, Galilee, and Samaria
Healing the sick and the lame and making the blind to see again!

Then I learned that he was crucified
And died on a cross for you and me,
But rose again on the third day,
For all the world to see!

So now I know I saw the "Savior",
When the star led us that way!
He was the "Christ", the "Son of God",
That we worshipped that blessed day!

SIMON PETER

I lived in Capernaum,
And had a house there that I made.
I lived there with my wife,
And was a fisherman by trade.

I had a brother named Andrew.
He was a fisherman like me.
We would go out together fishing,
On the Galilean Sea.

As John the Baptizer
Was baptizing by the Jordan River one day,
Andrew and his friend John came there,
Just to hear what he would say.

There with the Baptizer, Andrew met Jesus,
Thought he was the "Messiah" and wanted me to see!
I did not believe him at first,
For I thought, "How could this be!"
(John 1: 40-42)

After fishing all night and catching no fish
One night on the Galilean Sea,
Jesus told me to lower my net on the opposite side,
And after filling my net, Jesus said:" Follow me!"
(Matthew 4: 18-20; Mark 1: 16-18; Luke 5: 1-11)

So, I was ready to follow Jesus,
'Tho I did not fully understand,
How could he do the things he did,
For he was just a man!

Now living with us in Capernaum
Was the mother of my wife.
She was very ill and about to die,
But Jesus touched her hand and brought her back to life!
(Mark 1: 29-31; Luke 4: 38-39)

One day when Jesus went to Cana,
To a wedding feast to dine,
There I saw a great miracle,
When Jesus turned water into wine!
(John 2: 1-11)

After that, Jesus did many miracles,
Healing the sick and the lame and making the blind to see!
Now I was convinced he was the "Christ",
The "Messiah", the "Savior" for you and me!
(Matthew 4: 23-25, 14: 34-36, 15: 29-31; Mark 1: 32--34)

For three years I followed Jesus
As he travelled far and near,
And I witnessed his many miracles,
And there were many stories for us to hear.

One night as Jesus was on the shore,
And we were on a boat on the Galilean Sea,
The weather was stormy, the water rough,
And a figure was walking on the water! Who could it be?

When I saw it was Jesus I said, "Call to me,
And I will walk on water too!"
So I got out of the boat and began to walk,
It looked quite easy to do!

But then I noticed the stormy sea,
And from Jesus my eyes turned away!
Then I began to sink and cried out
For help from Jesus that day!

Then Jesus reached out his hand
And pulled me from the stormy sea,
Back to the boat
Where I would safely be!
(Matthew 14: 22-33; Mark 6: 45-52)

One day, I went to the mountain with Jesus, James, and John.
There with Moses and Elijah, Jesus's face shone like the sun,
And the voice of God came down from heaven,
And said, "Jesus is my Son!"
(Matthew 17: 1-8; Mark 9: 2-8)

"Who do you say that I am?"
Jesus asked of me one day.
"You are the Messiah, the Son of the Living God", I said.
He replied, "You are correct in what you say!"

Then Jesus called me "Peter" and the "Rock",
And told me what He would do:
On this "Rock" He would build His Church,
And give me the keys to the Kingdom of Heaven too!
(Matthew 16: 13-20)

At the Last Supper in Jerusalem
I did not think Jesus should wash my feet,
But Jesus insisted and humbled himself,
Before He returned to His seat!
(John 13: 3-17)

Then Jesus predicted that we would all scatter and flee
When danger would come one day!
But I assured him that I would be faithful,
For that was the only way!
(Matthew 26: 30-35: Mark 14: 26-31; Luke 22: 31-34; John 13: 31-38)

In the Garden of Gethsemane
When soldiers tried to arrest my Lord,
I tried to defend against them,
And cut off one's ear with my sword!
(Matthew 26: 50-52; Luke 22: 49-51; John 18: 10-11)

When Jesus is taken to the house of the High Priest,
I follow them there that day,
But when a woman said I was a follower of Jesus,
I denied three times what she did say!
(Matthew 26: 69-75; Mark 14: 66: 72; Luke 22: 54-62)
(John 18: 15-18, 25-27)

When Jesus was crucified
There was not much we could do!
But when Mary told us Jesus had risen from the dead,
I ran to the tomb to see if it was true!

On entering the tomb, there was no one there,
Just a cloth where his body had been!
But I did not fully understand until I met my risen Lord,
That this was not the end!
(Luke 24: 9-12; John 20: 1-10)

After Pentecost my life began anew,
Telling all who Jesus was, and what my Lord had said,
Of all the teachings, and his miracles,
 And his rising from the dead!

Then Christians began being persecuted,
And I was imprisoned too,
But freed when chains fell from off my wrist,
And following an angel, I knew what to do!
(Acts 12: 1-11)

And so I preached the gospel of my Risen Lord
Until at last, I too was crucified,
And I know I had my faults and at times I failed,
But with my faith, I can always say - "I tried!"

JOSEPH

Luke 2: 1-21; Matthew 1: 18-22, 2: 1-12, 13-14, 19-23

My name is Joseph and I live in Nazareth.
By trade, I am a carpenter.
In that town lives a young girl named Mary,
And I am betrothed to her!
(Luke 1: 26-27)

I am proud of my royal heritage,
For I am from King David's royal line.
And Mary has that same royal background.
I'm glad that she will soon be mine.
(Matthew 1: 1-17: Luke 3: 23-28)

I have some children,
By a wife that has passed away.
And I'm looking forward to starting a new life,
With Mary as my wife one day

But then I hear that Mary is with child,
And I know not by me.
I could put her away quietly,
So my friends would not see.
(Matthew 1: 18-19)

Then one night I had a dream,
And an angel spoke to me.
I was told the child was of God.
And this was meant to be:

That I should take Mary as my wife
And give "Jesus" as the child's name.
For he will save his people from their sins
And the world will never be the same.

So I awoke and followed the word of God.
And planning for our new life,
I accepted Mary and this Holy Child
And took Mary for my wife.
(Matthew 1: 18-25)

Before the time for the birth of our child,
A Decree went out from Rome,
That all should be counted and taxed,
And each had to return to their ancestral home.
(Luke 2: 1-20)

So with Mary, my espoused wife,
Along the Jorden River we went,
The ninety or so miles to Bethlehem,
To the ancestral home of our descent.

And Mary, being great with child,
On a donkey's back she rode
The four- or five-days trip,
With all the others on the road.

We finally arrived in Bethlehem,
A small village now packed for the census.
The inns were all full and we knew no one there,
 But an innkeeper had pity on us!

So we were allowed to stay in a stable,
Which fulfilled what the Prophets did say,
"That a virgin would give birth to a child in Bethlehem",
When Mary gave birth to our child that day!
(Isaiah 7: 14; Micah 5: 2)

And we wrapped the babe in swaddling clothes,
And in a manger, there was laid.
So this child was born,
 And the angels of God we had obeyed.

While we were there,
Shepherds came,
To pay homage to this Child of God,
And they worshipped and praised his Holy Name!
(Luke 2: 8-20)

We Christened this boy and named him "Jesus",
As the Angel Gabriel had told me to do!
And I raised him up to be a man,
And taught him carpentry skills too!
(Luke 2: 21)

While still in a house in Bethlehem, perhaps at the age of two,
Wisemen from the East also came,
Bringing gifts of gold, frankincense, and myrrh,
And they worshipped His Holy Name!
(Matthew 2: 9-11)

Then warned in a dream by an angel,
To take the child and Mary and flee,
For Herod was seeking to destroy this child,
So to Egypt we went to safely be!
(Matthew 2: 13-15)

And there we lived,
Until Herod was dead,
And again, the angel appeared,
"Arise and go to Israel", is what the angel said.
((Matthew 2: 19-23)

So I took the child and Mary,
Back to Nazareth and my home,
And raised this boy as my son,
And never more did I roam.

But I did travel each year to Jerusalem,
Being there for Passover week,
And once Jesus, at age 12, stayed behind in the Temple,
Where to the religious teachers he would speak!
(Luke 2: 41-52)

So this boy of mine and Child of God,
Grew in wisdom and statue, and with favor of God and man!
And 'tho I knew he was the Son of God,
There was still a lot I did not understand!
(Luke 2: 52)

Although I didn't live to see him teach,
Or perform the miracles that he did,
I know he was the "Messiah",
And would do what the Lord would bid!

THE 12 DISCIPLES OF JESUS

Jesus chose 12 Disciples,
That He selected among all men.
What was important is that He chose **them,**
It didn't matter what they had been!

Simon and Andrew, James and John,
Were fishermen on the Galilean Sea.
They dropped their nets and followed Jesus,
When Jesus said, **"Follow me!"**
(Matthew 4: 18-22)

Andrew was the brother of Simon,
And told Simon **"Jesus is the One!"**
That was the role of Andrew,
To bring Simon to God's Only Son!
(John 1: 41)

Jesus changed Simon's name to "Peter",
And calling him "The Rock", Jesus would say:
"On this my Rock I will build my church,
And give you the keys to Heaven one day!"
(Matthew 16: 16-19)

James and John were sons of Zebedee,
Who Jesus called, "Sons of Thunder!"
"In Glory, who would sit at Jesus' right hand",
Is what these brothers would wonder!
(Mark 10: 35-37)

Matthew was a tax collector for Rome.
At his taxing booth one day,
Jesus told Matthew to follow Him, and he did,
To see what Jesus would do and say!
(Matthew 9: 9)

Phillip, like Andrew and Peter, was from the town of Bethsaida,
And when Jesus left for Galilee,
He found Phillip,
And simply said, **"Follow me!**
(John 1: 43-44)

Phillip was a friend of Nathaniel[8],
And told him of Jesus one day.
"Can anything good come out of Nazareth?'
Was the first thing that Nathaniel did say!
(John 1: 45-46)

"Come see", said Phillip and they met Jesus,
Who told Nathaniel, "I saw you under the tree!"
Then Nathaniel knew Jesus was the Christ,
And cried out, "Rabbi, Son of God" and knew it was He!
(John 1: 45-49)

Jesus went up on a mountain to pray one day.
Staying all night at sunrise He came down,
And calling all His disciples together,
Chose 12 Apostles[9] from all those gathered 'round!
(Luke 6: 1`2-16)

When Jesus threatened to go to Judea,
Where the Jews had threatened to Him stone,
Thomas said, "Lets us go with Him and also die",
For He should not die alone!
(John 11: 7-8; 16)

Now this is the same "doubting" Thomas,
Who did not believe Jesus did rise,
But exclaimed, "My Lord and my God",
When he saw the risen Jesus with his own eyes[10]!
(John 20: 24-29)

---

[8] Nathaniel was the Disciple of Jesus called "Bartholomew."
[9] The names of the 12 Apostles chosen by Jesus were: Simon (Who He named Peter), Andrew (Peter's brother), James and John (who were brothers), Phillip, Bartholomew, Matthew, Thomas, James (the Less, son of Alphaeus), Simon (Who was called the Zealot), Judas (or Thaddeus or Jude, son of James), and Judas Iscariot (Who later betrayed Jesus)
[10] "He doubted that we might not doubt!", Augustine.

Judas Iscariot[11] was the treasurer of the 12,
Tho he was dishonest, Jesus always knew,
That Judas had a role to play,
And would do what he must do!
(John 12: 4-6, 6: 70, 13: 21-27)

The 11 Disciples met with Jesus several times,
After Jesus had risen from the dead.
He left with them the Holy Spirit,
And they remembered what He had taught and said!
(John 20: 19-22, 26-29, John 21: 1-14)

The Disciples came from various backgrounds and professions,
Each brought something to them all!
Jesus chose each one for a reason,
And each would answer Jesus' call!

They heard His teachings and his stories,
And watched as He performed miracles too!
They learned to believe He was the "Christ",
And knew what they would have to do!
(Matthew 16: 13-20; Mark 8: 27-30: Luke 9: 18-20)

So the 11 went to Galilee to the mountain,
In response to Jesus' call,
And there He gave them the "Great Commission",
To go to all nations preaching the "Good News" to one and all!
(Matthew 28: 16-20)

---

[11] After his betrayal of Jesus, Judas hanged himself because of his guilt and remorse. (Matthew 27: 3-5)

THE PARALYTIC MAN

John 5: 1-9, 14

At the Pool of Bethesda

In the Gospel of John
We can read this day,
The 3rd miracle of Jesus
That occurred this way:

There was a pool of water,
In the City of Jerusalem
Where people lame and blind
Would around there come.

It was said an angel,
Would stir the waters there,
And the first to enter,
Their ills no longer would bear!

So there a paralytic man
For 38 years did lay,
Upon his mat in hopes
Of there being cured one day.

That day a man named Jesus came,
As all good Jews should do,
To a festival in Jerusalem,
And approached those waters too.

Jesus saw the man,
Lying there upon his bed.
"Do you want to be made well?"
To him Jesus said.

But the man just pondered,
And offered this excuse:
"No one is here to help me,
So, what's the use!"

"Take up your mat and walk!"
Was Jesus's next reply.
So, the man got up and left,
Without a thanks or goodbye!

But in the Temple
They would meet again,
And Jesus said, "You are well!
Go and do not sin!"

So, the man went away,
And the story ends.
The man was cured that day,
And washed from his sins!

So, we see an end,
To John's 3rd sign,
Which signs began in Cana,
When Jesus turned water into wine!

THE SEVEN SIGNS
OF JOHN'S GOSPEL

In John we see the seven signs,
Of whom Jesus really is,
The Christ, the Messiah, the Son of God,
All these titles that are His!

At a wedding in Cana,
The host was in a bind!
So Mary turned to Jesus,
And He turned water into wine![12]

In Capernaum lay a dying boy,
The Royal Official's son.
He begged Jesus to come and cure,
But just with words, it was done![13]

At the Pool of Bethesda, lay a crippled man,
And Jesus came by one day.
"Take up your mat and walk", He said,
And the man jumped up and walked away![14]

As Jesus preached on a mountain one day,
There were 5,000 people there.
"How to feed them", the Disciples asked.
But five loaves and two fish made plenty to share![15]

Out on the sea, a storm comes up.
The ship is about to sink!
Upon the water Jesus walks,
And saves them from the brink![16]

---

[12] First Sign: John 2: 1-11
[13] Second Sign: John 4: 43-54
[14] Third Sign: John 5: 1-15
[15] Fourth Sign: John 6: 1-14
[16] Fifth Sign: John 6: 1-21

Along the road a man born blind,
Hears Jesus come his way.
He calls to Jesus to make him well,
And he was made to see that day![17]

In a certain town, a man lay ill.
"Jesus! Come, without delay!"
But Jesus waits two days for the "Glory of God",
Before He began on His way.

"My brother would not have died,
If you had come that day!"
But **"I Am, the Resurrection and the Life",**
To Martha Jesus then did say!

So they go to the tomb,
And Jesus weeps and begins to pray!
"Come Out!" He cries, and Lazarus comes out –
Alive to live another day![18]

John gave these signs,
For all the world to see,
That Jesus is the Christ, the Son of God,
A Savior for you and me!

---

[17] Sixth Sign: John 6: 1-6
[18] Seventh Sign: John 11: 1-44

A FEW SELECTED DAILY DEVOTIONALS

I wrote the small collection of Daily Devotionals that follows in response to a challenge from our Pastor, (Reverend Doctor Randy Lucas, Highlands United Methodist Church, Highlands, North Carolina}, to a small group of church members who were meeting on Zoom during the Covid "lockdown" every Sunday morning before our church services. In these sessions we talked about the daily readings from the previous week of "The Upper Room," a religious Christian publication of daily devotionals published out of Nashville, Tennessee. In one of our sessions, our Pastor suggested that we each write something similar. I met this challenge by eventually writing some daily devotionals in the format of "The Upper Room," but with some changes to reflect my own style. I presented this collection of some thirty or so daily devotionals to my wife on our 60th wedding anniversary. These are the Daily Devotionals I have included herein.

NOAH AND THE ARK

Genesis 6: 11--22

So Noah did everything God commanded of him.
Genesis 6: 22 (NLT)

Among my hobbies I like to carve. I will take a block of wood and carve an animal, a bird, a figure, or a caricature. Since our home is in the mountains, we have named our home, "Fox Run," so I have carved several small fox figures. I have also carved a Cardinal Redbird, a Chic-a dee, and an Owl. Over the years I have also carved figures or caricatures of pastors I have had and liked, all in their robes and vestments, holding Bibles, some standing behind wooden pulpits with paper sermons, and I have presented these to the various pastors in appreciation for their dedication and service to the Lord.

One of the first things I created and carved years ago was a Noah's Ark with a hand-crafted wooden ark and carved figures of Noah, his wife, and the animals. I had hand carved two each of elephants, giraffes, lions, camels, sheep, cows, pigs, hippopotami, and goats and topped the ark off with a small carved dove. Kids loved to play with the animals, and it reminded us all of that story in Genesis.

The sixth chapter of that book sets out in detail that story, and whether the story is true or not, it is nevertheless important to demonstrate God's power, justice, mercy, love, and compassion for those who are faithful and love the Lord. So we might use the analogy to say that God loves us so much that He sent his own "Ark" in the form of His only Begotten Son, Jesus Christ, to rescue us from our sins and transgressions.

Thought for the Day: Get aboard God's "Ark of Love!"

Prayer: *Heavenly Father, thank you for sending your Son as an "Ark" to rescue us from our sins and wickedness. Help us to be faithful servants so that we might come aboard. Amen.*

THE BREAD OF LIFE

John 6: 31-35

Then Jesus declared, "I am the bread of life."
John 6: 35 (NIV)

My wife loves to bake bread. The aroma of her bread baking in the oven is heavenly. But the taste of warm freshly baked bread with butter and jam is even better!

Bread has always been a beloved staple food, even in Biblical times, and is mentioned throughout both the Old and New Testaments. In the Book of Exodus, we read of God sending down bread of heaven, the "manna," which sustained the Israelite children daily as they wandered for forty years in search of the Promised Land, (Exodus 16: 4, 35) And in the Old Testament we see bread being served as nourishment as by Ruth, Esau, Elijah, and many others.

In the New Testament we read of Jesus feeding the 5,000 with just five loaves of bread and two fish, with baskets of crumbs left over. (Matthew 14: 13-21) But with Jesus we see that bread is more than just nourishment, and bread is given a greater significance. Jesus tells us that, "Man cannot live by bread alone" (Matthew 4:4) and declares that "I am the bread of life, and whoever comes to me will never be hungry." (John 6: 35) And then at the Last Supper we see that bread becomes the body of Christ. (Luke22: 19) So let us eat it in remembrance of our Lord and Savior Jesus Christ.

Thought for the Day: Take and eat in remembrance of Jesus Christ.

Prayer: *Dear Lord, give us this day the "Bread of Life" that comes from Heaven and gives life to us all. Amen.*

HERE'S THE CHURCH

1 Corinthians 14: 26

"For where two or more are gathered together in my name,
there I am in the midst of them."
Matthew 18: 20 (KJV)

When our children were small, we would play a little hand game with them and say the rhyme, "Here's the church and here's the steeple. Open the door and see all the people." It was fun for them and perhaps an easy step in learning about the church.

As adults, we learn that the "church" is more than just a building, although we also learned we could always find God there. But we also learned that the "church" is the communion and fellowship of Christian believers in the presence of God.

Although the selected scripture above originally referred to prayer, I think it equally applies, in sentiment, to the church when it says that where two or more people are gathered in His name, God is there among them. (paraphrased)

I liked the song we sang as a youth that said," I am the church! You are the church! We are the church together! All who follow Jesus, all around the world, we are the church together!"

The Apostle Peter reminded us (1 Peter 2: 5) that we, the people, the saints, are the lively building stones of the House of God, in a spiritual sense. Yes, we are the church! Thanks be to God!

Thought for the Day: We are the church!

Prayer: *Loving Father, Thank you for the church. Help us to be the church you would have us to be. Amen.*

ABOVE THE CLOUDS

Exodus 13: 21 and 16: 10

Thy mercy, O Lord is in the heavens, and thy faithfulness reaches unto the cloud.
Psalms 36: 5 (KJV)

Early each Sunday morning during the Covid lockdown, our Pastor[19] had what he called his "Upper Room Sunday School Class." A small group of us would meet on Zoom and discuss that day's "Upper Room" devotional reading, as well as any other readings that were particularly meaningful or spoke to any one of us the previous week.

On one Sunday someone mentioned a devotional that touched on the importance of spending time with God. During our discussion, our Pastor asked if any of us had a special place where we might feel particularly close to God. Another member said her "special place" was a particularly beautiful mountain vista which changed with the various seasons and weather. There were times, she said, when the clouds "rolled in" and covered the base of the mountains and the landscape below, but above the clouds it was clear and there she could feel closer to God.

In scripture, God sometimes appears in the clouds and there you see His glory. (Exodus 13: 24 and 16: 10) But above the clouds, you can see Heaven more clearly and perhaps have a "Mountaintop Experience"', that momentous happening that stays with you and perhaps changes your life.

In Memphis, Tennessee on April 3, 1968, the Rev, Dr. Martin Luther King, Jr. gave a speech entitled, "I've Been to the Mountain". In that speech Dr. King said, "He's allowed me to go to the mountaintop. And I've looked over and I've seen the Promised Land, … I may not get there with you… But… mine eyes have seen the glory of the coming of the Lord."

---

[19] Pastor Randy Lucas, Highlands United Methodist Church, Highlands, North Carolina

Thought for the Day: Where do you feel close to God?

Prayer. *Dear God, thank you for giving us special places where we might feel closer to you, places where we might feel your peace and love and behold your glory. Amen.*

A LIFE CHANGING DAY

Mark 2: 1-12

"I tell you, get up, take up your mat and go home."
Mark 2: 11 (NIV)

At 82 years of age, I broke my first bone, my right ankle in a slip and fall accident. I never realized how crippling and disabling a broken bone could be. I have had three casts and for almost four months I had been unable to drive, walk or put any pressure or weight on that foot! So, sitting and thinking, I thought of how lonely, and disabled was the paralytic man in our scripture quoted above. I am sure he was often ignored or pitied and could only just sit on his mat and beg.

But this paralytic had friends, and in Capernaum where they all lived, they had heard of this man named "Jesus" who had preached of love and had healed the sick, the blind, and the lame. And they had faith that this Jesus could help our paralytic too! And although the crowds were great, the friends lowered him through the roof to Jesus below. And Jesus saw their faith, and had compassion, and forgave the man of his sins, and told him to take up his mat and go home. And the man was healed and picked up his mat and went away. But I can imagine that he praised God, and Jesus, and his friends every day for the miracle that changed his life forever!

Thought for the Day: Jesus heals!

Prayer: *Merciful God, thank you for the healing power of Jesus, who not only forgives our sins, but heals the sick, the blind, and the lame. Thanks be to God! Amen.*

THE BIBLE IN A "NUTSHELL"

John 3: 16

... God is love
1 John 4: 8 (KJV)

I can remember very well some early memories as a child of my Sunday School Class. My teacher was a kind, elderly lady who seemed to love all us kids and shared with us Bible stories and her love of God. She told us about Noah and the Ark, David and Goliath, Jonah and the whale, and other such simple well-known stories that made us want to come back for more, and made us love her, the class, and begin to love and learn about the Bible, Jesus, and God. Each week she would bring us a new Bible verse and encourage us to learn it if we could. The first of these I think I remember was, "God is love." Another was John 3: 16. These two, I think, are the simplest and most basic statements of what the Bible and God are all about.

Sometimes later I would add the "Golden Rule", Do unto others as you would have them do unto you. (Paraphrased, Matthew 7: 12) And to round out I must add the "First and Greatest Commandment": "Love the Lord your God with all your heart and with all your soul, and with all your mind", and the "Second": "Love your neighbor as yourself." (Matthew 22: 37-39) All that remains is the story of the death of Jesus on the cross for the redemption of our sins, and His resurrection. (Matthew 27: 32-50 and 28: 1-10)

Taken as a whole, these verses, to me, tell the story of the Bible in a nutshell!

Thought for the Day: God is Love!

Prayer: *Dear Lord, thank you for Sunday Schools teachers who share their love of God, Jesus and the Bible. Give them the wisdom to impart your word and help their students to understand and appreciate what is being taught to them. Amen.*

TALENTS

1 Peter 4: 10-11

Having gifts that differ according to the grace given us, let us use them.
Romans 12: 6 (RSV)

As an adult, my Sunday School teacher was an ordained minister who had left the ministry for a career in education. Because of his theological background his lessons were always inspiring and thought provoking. After twenty-six years as our teacher however, he retired from his life's work and moved to the mountains to enjoy retirement. To keep our small little class of about twenty going, I agreed, along with three others, to teach our Sunday School Class one Sunday a month, although I was reluctant because I had never taught Sunday School before.

After a few months, my wife and I were celebrating our 50th wedding anniversary and we had invited the members of our Sunday School Class to join us in our celebration at a nice local restaurant. At the end of the dinner one-member told the group to remember that I was teaching our class the following Sunday. Suddenly, another member shouted out in a loud voice, **"Oh No!"** Everyone laughed and I was relieved when that member explained that he was disappointed because he and his wife were going to be out of town Sunday and would miss my "fine lesson".

Some of us are musically gifted, others artistic or creative, others have the ability to speak, or are skilled mechanically. Some can pray, some can teach, some can write cards, others can visit the lonely and shut ins. We are all born with different and distinct gifts and talents. God expects us to use whatever of those gifts and talents we might have to serve others and in doing so glorify God.

Thought for the Day: Do not hide your talents!

Prayer: *Heavenly Father, we thank you for the gifts and talents that we each have received. Help us to use these to serve others and in doing so glorify God. Amen.*

COMPANY'S COMING

Matthew 7: 7-11

"…knock and it shall be opened unto you."
Matthew7: 8 (KJV)

In our 60 years of marriage, my wife and I have had eight Cocker Spaniel dogs. Our current Cocker is a pretty, little black and white female we call "Bree". Bree loves everyone and is the friendliest Cocker we have had. She gets especially excited when company, friends, and family come for a visit. She has come to expect that a knock on the door means that company is coming, and she thinks they are coming just to see her.

Now, at almost three, when we are hurrying around the kitchen or are busy setting the table, Bree has come to expect that company is coming, and she will go sit by the front door, patiently waiting for that knock on the door.

In both the Gospels of Matthew and Luke, we see Jesus telling his disciples, "Knock and the door will be opened to you", speaking figuratively about opening to God in prayer. In the Gospel of John 14: 13, Jesus goes on to say, "If you ask any thing in my name, I will do it."

So, just as a little dog anxiously awaits the knock on the door for the company that is coming, so too does God await our prayers of supplication – knocking, and the door will be opened to us; asking, and our Lord will answer – perhaps not always in the way we might hope or expect, but in a way that we know that God understands, and that He is there for us in our time of need, to hold and comfort us and give us strength to get through any problem we might have!

Thought for the Day: God is ready to hear our prayers.

Prayer: Gracious Lord, as we ask and seek and knock upon your door in your name, let us find comfort and strength in our problems, knowing you are there for us in our time of need. Amen

IT IS FINISHED

John 19: 17-19

When Jesus had received the vinegar, he said, "It is finished
and bowed his head and gave up his spirit.
John 19: 30 (RSV)

My wife is very artistic and crafty. She loves to sew, pleat little dresses, quilt, paint in watercolor, acrylic and oil, and hook rugs. Her current favorite of these is hooking. She will take a piece of pure linen, place it on a wooden frame, and with patterns she has drawn, begin hooking strips of wool of all colors, many of which she has dyed herself, into a beautiful rug, pillow, or hanging piece. It may take her several weeks or even months to complete an 8 x 10 rug of beautiful wildflowers of all colors on a black background. When she has finally completed her hooked piece, she will announce to all with great satisfaction, "It is finished!"

When Jesus was crucified, the various Gospels report seven different sayings of Jesus from the cross. The last, as reported in the Gospel of John has Jesus crying out as he breathed his last breath, "It is finished!" But these words were not intended by Jesus to indicate his life on earth was finished, although it was. Rather, they were intended to indicate that his work and life's mission here on earth had come to an end. He had lived an exemplary life, had performed miracles, healed the sick, made the blind to see and the lame to walk, raised the dead to life, all demonstrating his divine authority as the Son of God. He had shown us the loving and forgiving nature of God and he had suffered and died upon the cross for the forgiveness of the sins of mankind. He had accomplished what he came upon the earth to do. Yes, it was finished, and he had left a legacy for the world's greatest religion.

Thought for the Day; It is finished! He is risen!

Prayer: *Eternal God, thank you for sending your Son to show us your love and forgiveness and how to live and serve others. Amen.*

CARPENTRY

Philippians 2: 6-8

Isn't this the carpenter's son?
Matthew 13: 55 (NIV)

My wife and I lived in Virginia for a few years when I was in the military service. While we were there, we were able to visit Colonial Williamsburg on many occasions and fell in love with the style of colonial homes. Later, we designed and built a traditional colonial style house, complete with all types of crown, dental, ceiling and wall molding, inside and out, carefully crafted by skilled carpenters.

Jesus was known as the carpenter from Galilee, and he had learned this trade and his carpentry skills, no doubt, from his carpenter father. Carpentry then, was a difficult job that required a great deal of strength and endurance, as well as physical skills. All this demonstrated the humanity of Jesus. Although he was divine, he was also human and lived his early life as a common man who humbled himself to be the servant of mankind, and obedient to the will of his Heavenly Father, even to the point of death on the cross. This carpenter from Galilee became the "Master Builder", the builder of the Church, the Temple, (being you and me), and with the Holy Spirit being God within us!

Thought for the Day: Jesus, the divine and humble, obedient carpenter.

Prayer: Dear Lord, thank you for your Son, Jesus Christ, who humbled himself as a craftsman and a servant to mankind, and who was obedient to his Heavenly Father, even to the point of death on the cross. We pray the prayer your Son taught us, "Our Father, which art in heaven, hallowed be thy name. Thy kingdom come. Thy will be done in earth, as it is in heaven. Give us this day our daily bread. And forgive us our debts, as we forgive our debtors. And lead us not into temptation but deliver us from evil: For thine is the kingdom, and the power, and the glory, forever. Amen." (Matthew 6: 9-13, KJV)

GRADUATION

Proverbs 4:7

God is our refuge and strength, an ever-present help in trouble.
Psalms 46: 1 (NIV)

Our grandson graduated this year from college. Like so many other graduating students, he will be embarking on untraveled roads with new companions and new challenges and adventures. In fact, a week after graduation my grandson got married and two weeks later began embarking on a new career as a graphic designer with a large company.

For my grandson, and perhaps all graduates, it is a fresh start. Each day will have its rewards and challenges. But each day is also a precious gift from God. Every rising sun brings with it infinite possibilities. And with God on one's side, it is important that the most is made of each precious moment, and that contentment is found in whatever path one will travel. Life's road may at sometimes be difficult, but if one holds out one's hand, God will take it and provide the wisdom, comfort, and strength for any challenge or situation.

Thought for the Day: God is there for you.

Prayer: Lord Jesus, we ask your blessing upon all our graduating seniors. Let them feel your presence and know you are there for them and that each day provides a fresh start with unlimited opportunities. Amen.

GOD'S PLAN

Jonah 1: 16

My thoughts are not your thoughts. Your ways are not my ways.
Isiah 55: 8 (NCV)

On Palm Sunday my wife and I watched as our son, who is the Senior Pastor of his church, sang a carpella, "Were You There When They Crucified My Lord". He sang so beautifully, and we were so proud of him as an ordained minister, that tears almost came to our eyes.

My son was raised in the church and was always active. Growing up he participated in Sunday School, was an acolyte, and as a youth was active in the youth program and in the bell and youth choirs of our church.

We always suspected that he would someday become an ordained minister, so we were surprised when he decided to go to Law School and become a lawyer like his dad. But after the first year, he felt, "The Call", and decided on a double major in law and divinity. But after another year, now in divinity school, that "tug" was even greater, and my son dropped the idea of continuing with law all together and chose the ministry as his life's work and vocation.

Jonah had a plan of his own and chose, at first, not to follow God's directive, and even tried to flee from God. But God had other plans for Jonah, and we all know how that all came out.

In the Garden of Gethsemane, Jesus prayed, "Not my will, but thy will be done." (Matthew 14: 36, NIV)

We need to remember that God is in control!

Thought for the Day: God is in control!

Prayer: *Eternal God, help us to clearly see your will and your plan for our lives, as we pray, not my will, but thy will be done! Amen.*

CHALLENGES

1 Samuel 17: 32-50

I can do all things through Christ which strengtheneth me.
Philippians 4: 13 (KJV)

As a child you might say that I was shy. I was always quiet and was afraid of talking in public, even in high school and on into college. As I approached graduation from college, I was praying to God for guidance and direction for my future and felt a push to go to Law School and become a lawyer, which I did. Then as a young lawyer, I prayed to God for strength to be able to stand in front of a judge or jury and try a case. I found that strength and became a trial attorney, practicing 59 years before my recent retirement. The Lord had given me that strength and skill to make a successful career using public speaking.

David was but a young shepherd lad when he accepted the challenge to meet the head of the Philistine army. With the courage and strength from God, David was able with a sling and a few smooth stones to defeat the mighty Goliath who he then slew with Goliath's own sword. No matter how strong or daunting the obstacle, through the strength of Jesus Christ with the Lord by your side, you have the power and courage to overcome any challenge.

Thought for the Day: Fear not for God is with you.

Prayer: *Heavenly Father, thank you for being there for us to provide strength and courage in any of life's challenging situations. Amen.*

PIG IN THE ROAD

Distractions

Matthew 14: 25-33

Then when he saw the wind, he was afraid and beginning to sink,
cried out, "Lord save me!"
Matthew 14: 30 (NIV)

One day, before Covid, as my wife and I joined two other couples, we rode through some North Georgia rural roads just for the drive. While everyone was looking around and enjoying the scenery, my wife, who was sitting in the back of a large SUV, suddenly cried out, **"Pig in the road! Pig in the road!"** Everyone quickly returned their attention to the front to see in the middle of the road, quietly standing there, a very large pig, which our driver slowly and carefully drove around.

Years have gone by, and we still think at times of that drive, and laugh at the pig in the road. But this story reminds me too of the story in the Gospel of Matthew when Peter, in the midst of a storm, sees Jesus, walking on the water, and Peter gets out of the boat and begins walking himself on the water toward Jesus. So long as Peter keeps his eyes to the front and focused on Jesus, it is easy for him to do so, but when Peter looks away and sees the storm and the danger about him, he becomes afraid and begins to sink.

So, in our daily lives, as we become distracted with everything going on about us, we need to keep our eyes focused on Jesus, and He will reach out, comfort us, and bring us also back to the boat and to safety.

Thought for the Day: Keep your eyes on Jesus.

Prayer: Dear Lord, help us to keep our eyes focused on Jesus and trust Him to comfort and protect us when we become distracted. Amen.

DISAPPOINTMENTS

John 16: 33

Give all your worries to God because He cares for you.
1 Peter 5: 7 (NIV)

My wife recently came across a stack of letters I had written sixty plus years ago when I was at the Infantry Officers School at Fort Benning, Georgia. One letter recalled an incident when our platoon was expected to clean our barracks and have our cubicles and floor spotless for inspection each week. After every weekly inspection, our CO was angry when we came in third or fourth among the platoons in our company. So, my cubicle mate and I decided to spend our free time one evening recleaning the entire barracks after the platoon members had already done so. Unfortunately, the next morning despite two or three hours of extra cleaning, our platoon still came in third. Needless to say, we were disappointed, but the worst blow was that my cubical mate's and my cubicles received a few demerits for some deficiency.

Looking back, it reminds me that sometimes our best plans and intentions are met with disappointments, whether it will be in the workplace, in our relationships, love, marriage, or in any life situation, or in anything going on in our lives. Sometimes these disappointments are small, as was ours. But sometimes they may be significant. At these times, rather than let these disappointments fester and control our thoughts and emotions, we should instead, turn to God. Truly the best way to overcome disappointments in our lives is to go to God in worship and prayer, as did Job and David in their times of disappointment and loss. (See Job 1: 13-22 and 2 Samuel 12: 13-20)

Thought for the Day: God cares for you!

Prayer: *Loving God, when we are discouraged by disappointments in our lives, help us to come to you in prayer for strength and hope, knowing that you care for us. Amen.*

GENEALOGY

Matthew 1: 1-17

Jesus, Christ, the son of David, the son of Abraham.
Matthew 1: 1 (NIV)

One of my best friends is a genealogist, a person who traces or studies lives of family descent and ancestry. He had always been interested in genealogy, at first as a hobby, but when he retired early from his regular job, he began doing genealogy on a full-time basis and became a highly qualified professional genealogist. Over the years he has had many clients, and to prepare papers for them, he has travelled all over the country and even abroad to Ireland, Scotland, and Italy, to court houses, libraries, cemeteries, and private homes to gather, examine, and study all kinds of genealogical records. And he has even appeared on national television revealing the genealogy for certain well-known celebrities.

In the New Testament there are accounts of the genealogy of Jesus, one in the Gospel of Matthew (above), and another in the Gospel of Luke. (Luke 3: 23-38) Both go back through Joseph to David, Matthew on back to Abraham, Luke to Adam. Both Gospels place these accounts of ancestry of Jesus in the beginning of their Gospels to emphasize Jesus's entitlement to be called the long awaited "Messiah" – the "Anointed One", by being the "Son of David", a descendent of King David. And so, He is entitled to be called, the "Christ", the "Son of the Living God", God himself on earth in human form.

Thought for the Day: Jesus, the "Son of David."

Prayer: *Gracious Lord, thank you for sending your son to be the Messiah, God with us here on earth, for the redemption of our sins. Amen.*

SIGNS

John 11: 47

...Jesus did many other signs in the presence of the disciples...
John 20: 30 (NKJV)

As an Attorney and a Mediator I would often drive many miles through various counties to get to the court houses or to the different locations for my cases. As I did so I would pass many highway and directional signs pointing the way to my destination.

Of all the miracles of Jesus, (which the writer of the Gospel of John refers to as "signs",) that Gospel selects only seven of these as pointing, like signs, for the readers to understand who Jesus really is, that he is the "Christ", the "Messiah", "the Son of the living God" – in fact, "God Incarnate" – God in human form here on earth.

The selected "signs" (or miracles) in John's Gospel are: (1) Jesus turning water into wine at the wedding in Cana; (2) Jesus healing the Royal Official's son; (3) Jesus healing the paralytic man at the Pool of Bethesda; (4) Jesus feeding the 5,000 with only 5 loaves of bread and 2 fish; (5) Jesus walking on water; (6) Jesus healing the man born blind from birth; and (7) Jesus raising Lazarus from the dead.

All these signs demonstrated Jesus's divine authority to do miracles, with the results that the disciples "believed in Him". (John 2:11) And the writer of John's Gospel suggests that if we understand these 'signs", or (miracles), we too may believe and have eternal life, "... life in His name". (John 20: 31)

Thought for the Day: Believe!

Prayer: *Heavenly Father, although we may not have experienced the miracles of Jesus for ourselves, give us the understanding that by reading of the "signs" (miracles) in the Gospel of John, we too might believe and have eternal life. Amen.*

THE VINES

John 15: 1-12

"I am the vine; you are the branches."
John 15: 5 (NIV)

In the area where we live in the mountains of North Georgia there are several wineries. Each one is different, and as a tourist attraction we would visit each one over time, often taking friends or family members. Perhaps we have visited one more often because not only is it close to us, but it is set in a little valley surrounded by beautiful mountains, and on certain occasions they would serve pizza or chili to those visiting. We had also become acquainted with the owners of this one, and they had allowed us to walk the vineyards, had shown us their equipment, and explained how they pruned the vines and processed the grapes. In the spring they would invite us and the public to a special event where a local clergyman would bless the vines.

In the Bible, grapevines are mentioned more than any other plant. In the scripture quoted above, Jesus in the Gospel of John tells us the last of his seven "I am" sayings as he declares to us, "I am the vine, you are the branches." These were among the last words Jesus knew he would be telling his disciples before his crucifixion, so what he was telling them, to him, must have been important. If you read the rest of the words of Jesus on this occasion, both before and after the quoted scripture, you will understand that we are all dependent on Jesus, and are connected to and a part of Him, just as Jesus is connected to God. As such, we will bear "good fruit" to the glory of God.

Thought for the Day: We are connected to Jesus.

Prayer: *Creator God, thank you for allowing us as branches to be connected to Jesus, the vine, drawing our life from him, enabling us to bear "good fruit" to your glory. Amen.*

THE GARDEN

Genesis 2: 8-10

*I (Solomon) made me a garden and orchards and planted
trees in them of all kinds of fruits.*
Ecclesiastes 2: 5 (NIV)

My wife and I have always had a garden. When our children were little, we had a large vegetable garden of tomatoes, beans, corn, potatoes, squash, carrots, radishes, lettuce, and other crops. The kids liked to pick the fresh vegetables and even help work in the garden at times, and this made them appreciate and enjoy eating vegetables pulled fresh from our garden. When the kids grew up, my wife became a "Master Gardener" and spent hours working in a community garden that contributed hundreds of pounds of food to local poor and needy families.

In the Bible we read of a number of gardens. It all began in the Book of Genesis when God, the "Master Gardner", created a garden in Eden where he placed his man and woman. (See above referenced scripture) And in the Old Testament, we read of other gardens, as the Garden of Solomon, (See above quoted scripture) and in the New Testament the Garden of Gethsemane. (Matthew 26: 36) Some of these gardens were places of beauty, shelter, and shade. Others were places of solitude and retreat, or places to meet friends, talk and pray, as did Jesus in the Garden of Gethsemane with his disciples. (John 18: 1-2)

Thought for the Day: God is the "Master Gardener."

Prayer: *Father God, thank you for gardens that provide beauty and shade, places to relax, pray, and enjoy, and gardens that provide food to sustain life. Amen.*

MISTAKES

Psalms 119: 147

In my distress, I called upon the Lord.
Psalms 18: 6 (KJV)

My granddaughter's fiancée, one of seven children, recently told us a story about his mother, who on one occasion wanted to economize feeding her large family by buying some chickens for their eggs. She set out to purchase six hens and a rooster and came home with seven poulettes or young chicks. Excited about the possibilities, she created a nice coop for them, began to feed and watch them grow, expecting them to begin laying eggs in about eighteen weeks. After five months and no eggs, and six months and still no eggs, she sought advice from a local chicken farmer. To her surprise, she was told that she had seven roosters!

We all make mistakes in life, sometimes small, like buying roosters instead of hens, some more significant. The latter may involve relationships, marriage, the choosing of friends, financial decisions that result in loss, or any number of other life situations. Regarding the more significant mistakes in life, the important thing is not to let them build up inside, take over your thoughts and ruin your life. At these times, God is there for you. Turn to God in prayer, discuss your concerns with Him and listen for direction as to how to deal with these problems. There may be no easy solution, but you can let go, move on, and trust God, knowing that He will provide comfort and strength for you in dealing with these matters.

Thought for the Day: Trust God!

Prayer: *Dear Lord, when we make major mistakes in life which cause us great concern, help us to let go, move on, and turn to you for direction, comfort, and strength. Amen.*

LEAVEN

Matthew 13: 33

A little leaven leaveneth the whole...
Galatians 5: 9 (KJV)

My daughter loves to bake and is known for her delicious pound cakes. But I do remember an incident a few years ago when her baking just did not go as planned. She had carefully measured out the flour and other ingredients, mixed them together, and placed the cakepans with its batter in the oven, only to have them overrise and fail. She repeated the process a second and third time only to have the same results. Thinking something was wrong with her oven, she brought all the ingredients over to our house and tried again in our oven, only to have the same result for the fourth time. Hearing of her failures her mother asked her what type of flour she was using, and upon examination it was discovered that my daughter was using self-rising flour instead of plain flour as called for by the recipe. This caused the cake to overrise and fail. Too much leaven!

In the Bible, leaven is mentioned throughout both the Old and the New Testaments, often simply for its leavening quality which causes the dough to rise. Other times, leaven is symbolic of sin or evil, as when Jesus compares the false teachings of the Pharisees and Sadducees with leaven, (Matthew 16: 6-12) or with the evil of Herod. (Mark 8: 15) But at times, leaven could also be good, as when Jesus declared, "I am the bread of life", and compares leaven to the Kingdom of Heaven. (Matthew13; 33) Like the leaven put in the dough by the woman making bread, the gospel and the church may also start with a small beginning which can then spread and penetrate the whole of society until it is likened to the Kingdom of Heaven here on earth.

Thought for the Day: Jesus is the bread of life.

Prayer: *Faithful God, thank you that from a small beginning the gospel and the church may spread throughout the world. Amen.*

THE SHEPHERD

John 19: 1-21

The Lord is my shepherd, I shall not want...
Psalms 23: 1

Among the favorite places to travel for me and my wife are Ireland and Scotland. One of the reasons is their natural beauty with the hills dotted with sheep everywhere, seemingly unfenced and grazing loose, sometimes leisurely walking or lying in our roadway ahead. But occasionally, we would see a shepherd herding a flock of sheep down from the hills to greener pastures or the valleys below, again sometimes blocking the roadway ahead. Sometimes we would watch the sheepdogs round up the sheep and keep them in toe to the commands of the shepherds.

Back home, as I drove on occasions to a workplace destination, I would pass a field full of grazing sheep, guarded day and night by a beautiful white Great Pyrenees dog which served as their shepherd and protector.

Shepherds have served throughout history, even in Biblical times, to watch over and protect their flocks of sheep, and we read of them in both the Old and New Testaments. In Isiah 63: 11, Moses was called the "Shepherd "of his flock, the Israelite people. In 1 Samuel 17, we read of David, as a young shepherd boy who meets and slays Goliath. And we read that "the Lord is my shepherd..." in the 23rd Psalm. Then with the coming of Jesus, we think of Jesus as the "Good Shepherd", who lays down his life for us, his flock, for the redemption of our sins. (John 10: 11)

Thought for the Day: Jesus is the Good Shepherd!

Prayer: *Loving God, thank you for being our Shepherd to watch over and protect us, and for sending your Son, Jesus Christ, to be the Good Shepherd to also watch over and protect us and save us from our sins. Amen.*

THE BLACKSMITH

Philippians 4: 10-18

I can do all things through Christ who strengthens me.
Philippians 4: 13 (NKJV)

I recently came across a poem by Henry Wadsworth Longfellow entitled, "The Village Blacksmith". The poem begins this way: "Under a spreading chestnut tree the village smithy stands; The smith a mighty man was he, with large and sinewy hands, and the muscles of his brawny arms are strong as iron bands." To be a blacksmith you had to have great strength to pound with a heavy hammer on an iron anvil a red, hot, flaming rod tempered on a flaming forge. My wife and I have seen this strength demonstrated as we travelled to blacksmith shops in such historic places as Colonial Williamsburg, Old Sturbridge Village, and Shaker Village in Pleasant Hill, Kentucky.

In the Bible we see similar demonstrations of physical strength, as by Solomon when he slew thousands of the enemy with the single jawbone of a donkey. (Judges 15: 16) But in the New Testament, with the coming of Jesus, we see a different kind of strength, a strength that gives us courage to face a critical situation, like a bad relationship or a divorce, to get through a destructive act of nature, or to be content, accept, endure, or fight through a crippling injury or disease. Jesus Christ gives us the courage and the strength to do and endure all things.

Thought for the Day: Look to Jesus for strength.

Prayer: *Loving Father, we thank you for sending Jesus to comfort and strengthen us in all those times when we need courage and strength to face challenging, difficult, and fearful situations in our lives. Amen.*

MUSIC

Psalms 150: 1-6

Make a Joyful noise to the Lord, come into his presence with singing.
Psalms 100: 1-2 (ESV)

I have always liked and enjoyed music. Beginning in elementary school I was given a trumpet and began taking lessons. I continued playing trumpet throughout high school and into college. When I started attending a church that had a bluegrass band, I took up the banjo and started taking lessons.

A favorite part of any church service to me is its music. I love to hear a piano, or an organ play a Bach or Christian hymn, and a church choir or soloist sing an old favorite or new selection. And nothing can get me "in the spirit" better than singing along with a favorite gospel or spiritual song by our bluegrass band.

Music of all kinds has long been used, even in Biblical times, in religious services as part of the worship of God and is mentioned in both the Old and New Testaments. In Genesis (4: 21) we see Jubal playing the lyre and pipe. In Exodus (15: 1-21) we see Moses and the Israelites singing a song to the Lord and playing timbrels for their victory and defeat of the Egyptian army. And we know of David's many psalms. And ending with the New Testament, after the Last Supper we read of Jesus and his disciples singing a hymn before going out to the Mount of Olives. (Matthew 26: 30)
Yes, music is a vital part of our worship of God!

Thought for the Day: Praise the Lord with music.

Prayer: *Loving God, thank you for music, for the playing of musical instruments and the singing of songs that help us to praise and worship and glorify your name. Amen.*

TEACHERS

Matthew 4: 23

When Jesus had finished saying these things the crowds
were amazed at his teachings.
Matthew 7: 28 (NIV)

Teachers have always been an important part of my life. My wife is a teacher, as is my daughter, daughter in law, granddaughter, and grandson's wife. Both my mother and father were teachers, as were four aunts.

The Disciples and many contemporaries of Jesus often referred to him as "Rabbi" or "Teacher". Of the ninety times that Jesus is addressed in the Bible, sixty of those he is referred to in this way. But Jesus never referred to himself in this manner, rather thinking of himself as the "Messiah", the "Christ", the "Son of Man", and the "Son of God". But Jesus was a teacher! He taught with words, he taught in parables, and he taught by his actions in his life, his ministry, his miracles, and in his acts of healing the sick, the lame, the blind, the lepers, and raising the dead to life. He taught one on one, he taught his Disciples, he taught crowds of 5,000 and many others. He taught in the mountains, in the valleys, by the seashore, off and in boats, in private homes, in the synagogues and tabernacles, by pools of water, by wells, and along the road. He taught in Galilee, Judea, Samaria, and elsewhere. He taught with divine authority, power, and compassion. Although Jesus never professed to be a teacher, he was the world's greatest teacher!

Thought for the Day: Live by the teachings of Jesus!

Prayer: O God, thank you for the teachings of Jesus that taught us how to live, how to love and serve God and our fellow man and this way glorify your Holy Name. Amen

LEFT BEHIND

Psalms 23:-6

"So do not fear, for I am with you…"
Isiah 41: 10 (NIV)

My wife was taking our little Cocker Spaniel dog for her morning walk along a neighborhood street when a deer, a pretty doe, darted to the right, across the street in front of them. As my wife looked back to the left, she noticed a small fawn that stood frozen on the opposite side of the street looking frightened, and longing to be with its mother. When the doe got a little distance away, it also stopped, and looked back longingly at the baby fawn. Then she turned away and darted toward the woods as if to say, "follow me!"

As my wife and little dog stood watching, the little fawn got up the courage to scamper across the road toward its mother, and both disappeared out of sight.

I am sure that little fawn knew that its mother was there for it, to love and protect it, and that it needed to follow her wherever she went.

This reminds me of how God, our Father, is also there for us, to love and protect us with His peace and strength, and we need to follow Him wherever He leads us.

Thought for the Day: God is there for us!

Prayer: *Dear Lord, thank you for your great love for us, your peace and protection! Lead us O Lord, show us the way and we will follow! Amen.*

NEIGHBORS

Luke 24: 13-35

Then their eyes were opened, and they recognized him...
Luke 24: 31 (NIV)

When I got out of the military service many years ago, we bought our first house and moved in. Over a period of months, we briefly met several of our new neighbors. I had also joined a civic club and one of its first excursions was a trip to a local airport where we toured a hanger and talked to some of the employees. One of these was a nice gentleman to whom I had introduced myself. I was surprised when he said, "I know who you are. I am your next-door neighbor." I was not only surprised, but quite embarrassed, but I simply did not recognize him in this setting from my first brief meeting with him and his wife.

In the Gospel of Luke, we read of Jesus, after his crucifixion and resurrection, encountering two fellow travelers on the road to Emmaus.
Although they had been disciples of Jesus, they did not recognize him until that evening as they broke bread together. Imagine their surprise and joy, for not only did they know this fellow traveler, but he was the same Jesus who had been crucified and died on the cross, who they had heard had risen from the dead and had now been walking and talking with them on the road to Emmaus. You can understand their excitement as they shared their good news and joy with the other disciples and followers of Jesus.

Thought for the Day: Will you recognize Jesus?

Prayer: *Gracious Lord, we thank you for the risen Christ. Help us to recognize Jesus as we encounter Him in our daily lives. In Jesus name we pray. Amen.*

FAITHFUL HEALING

Read John 4: 43-54

Jesus said to him, "Go, your son will live."
John 4: 50 (RSV)

My grandfather was a very devout Christian man. When I was young, I remember him telling my mother about his closest neighbor, who lived about half a mile away, who was critically ill with pneumonia and was reportedly not expected to live. Upon hearing this news, my grandfather told of how he prayed to God for the healing of this, his good friend. He told mother that the next day he received news that his friend had miraculously recovered, and at about the time he had prayed, and that his friend was now doing fine.

As I think back on this, I recall a similar story in the Gospel of John when the royal official comes to Cana in Galilee to beg Jesus to come back to Capernaum for the healing of his son. Instead of going the fifty or so miles to Capernaum to lay hands on the boy, as Jesus often did to heal those who were sick or infirm, Jesus simply told the royal official, "Go, your son will live." With faith, the royal official began returning to Capernaum when a servant met him on his journey and advised him that his son had recovered, and at about the same time Jesus had told him that his son would live. The royal official had faith! So did my grandfather! In both cases, those that were sick were healed at a distance without the laying on of hands.

Prayers for healing, even with faith, may not always be answered by God in the way we might ask or hope. But we can be confident that God hears our prayers and will be there for us, to comfort and strengthen us and those we pray for in the face of illness, sickness, and other needs.

Thought for the Day: God's word is sufficient to heal.

Prayer: Merciful God, give us the faith to pray for healing, knowing that your word is sufficient to heal the sick and infirm. Amen.

OUR ABC'S

Job 22: 22

*"Man shall not live on bread alone but on every word
that comes from the mouth of God."*
Matthew 4: 4 (NIV)

As little children we learn our ABC's. My Aunt, Elnora France, in 1966 wrote a little book just for the family entitled, **"Lets Learn Our Bible ABC's"**. The following is an excerpt:

A. *All things work for good to them that love God.* (Romans 8: 28).

B. *Be still and know that I am God.* (Psalms 46: 10).

C. *Cast all your cares upon him, for he careth for you.* (! Peter 5: 7).

D. *Depart from evil and do good.* (Psalms 37: 27).

E. *Enter into his gates with thanksgiving, and into his courts with praise.* (Psalms 100: 4).

F. *Forgive us our trespasses as we forgive those who trespass against us.* (Matthew 6: 12).

G. *God is love.* (1 John 4: 8).

H. *Have faith in God,* (Mark 11: 22).

I. *It is a good thing to give thanks unto the Lord.* (Psalms 92: 1).

J. *Judge not that you be not judged.* (Matthew7: 1).

K. *Knock and it shall be opened unto you.* (Matthew 7: 7).

L. *Lo, I am with you always.* (Matthew 28: 20).

M. *Make a joyful noise unto the Lord all ye lands.* (Psalms 100: 1).

N. *Neither do I condemn you… Go and sin no more.* (John 8: 11).

O. *O Lord how great are thy works.* (Psalms 92: 5).

P. *Pray without ceasing.* (1Thessalonians 5: 17).

Q. *Quench not the spirit.* (1Thessalonians 5: 19).

R. *Remember the Sabbath to keep it holy.* (Exodus 20: 8).

S. *Surely, goodness and mercy shall follow me all the days of my life.* (Psalms 23: 6).

T. *The Lord is my shepherd; I shall not want.* (Psalms 23: 1).

U. *Understanding is a wellspring of life unto him that hath it.* (Proverbs 16:22).

V. *Verily, I say unto you, inasmuch as ye did not to one of the least of these, ye did it not to me.* (Matthew 25: 45).

W. *We are laborers together with God.* (1 Corinthians 3: 9).

X. *Except a man be born again, he cannot see the Kingdom of God.* (John 3: 5).

Y. *Ye are the light of the world, a city set on a hill cannot be hidden.* (Matthew 5:14).

Z. *Zion heard and was glad.* (Psalms 97: 8).

Thought for the Day: To read the Bible is to know God.

Prayer: *God our Father, help us to read the Bible daily, and by so doing, understand your message for our lives. Amen.*

MARY

Luke 2: 6-7

"… Truly I tell you, whatever you did for one of the least of these brothers and sisters of mine, you did for me."
Matthew 25: 40 (NIV)

One December morning as I was driving to work, a young woman who was advanced with child was standing near a stop sign holding a sign that read, "Please help!". I came to the stop sign, then drove on, looking straight ahead. But as I drove on, I started thinking of that young woman and what the sign said. I also started thinking of another young woman who, with her husband, had tried to find a place to stay in a little town called Bethlehem. Although there was no room to be found, an innkeeper gave them a place to stay … in a stable.!

So, as I drove the same way the next morning, this time I stopped and smiled and handed her a bill. She smiled back and said, "God bless you!"

As I continued to drive that way each morning, I would raise my hand and smile as I passed, and she would smile and wave right back.

Then one day as I drove by, she was not there. I supposed she had delivered her child. But I guess she knew I cared!

In the parable of the sheep and the goats, in response to a question by the "righteous", Jesus said that he who serves his brother or sister, does it "unto me!"

Thought for the Day: In serving others, we serve God.

Prayer: Eternal God, open our eyes that we may see the needs of others and serve the least of these in your name! Amen.

THE FIRST CHRISTMAS

Luke 2: 1-21

For unto us a child is born, unto us a son is given.
Isiah 9: 6 (KJV)

Recently, as my wife and I were cleaning out our house, preparing to move our residence after my retirement to the North Georgia Mountains, we came across a lined elementary school manuscript paper entitled,
"The First Christmas" written by our son who was at that time a first grader.

The following, unedited, is exactly how he had written it:

"The First Christmas"
by Brian Germano

"A long tine ago an angel told mary that she was going to have a byby. That was going to be christ the lord. So mery went to Bethlehem. When they got there the Incepr said, sorry the rooms are all filled up. The only (over on the back) please I have is a stebl. We will take it. So, the Incepr led mery ans Josof to the stebl. Then a brit! brit! stare did show over Bethlehem. And that night, a byby was born. And mary named hem Jesus. the End" (sic)

But that was not "the End" Jesus and my son both grew in wisdom and statue and in favor of God and man!

My son is now an ordained minister and Senior Pastor of a 2,000-member church. And Jesus did reveal himself as Christ the Lord, and was called,
"… Wonderful, Counsellor, the Mighty God, the Everlasting Father, the Prince of Peace'! (Isiah 9:6) Thanks be to God!

Thought for the Day: Jesus Christ is born!

Prayer: *Heavenly Father, thank you for sending your son to be born as a babe in Bethlehem that first Christmas, Emanuel, God with us here on earth. Amen.*

ABOUT THE AUTHOR

Don Germano is a retired Attorney who lives in Sky Valley, in the Mountains of North Georgia. He is married to his wife, Sara Mac, of over sixty years. They have two children, their son, Brian, an ordained Methodist Minister serving in the North Georgia Conference of the United Methodist Church, and his daughter, Amy Tice, who works with her husband as an Interior Designer and resides in Augusta, Georgia. Don and his wife have three grandchildren and two great-granddaughters.

Don enjoys in retirement being with family and friends, his church, travelling, cooking, writing poetry, walking with his wife and their dog, reading history, and playing the banjo.